QUEEN ELIZABETH II

A CELEBRATION OF HER LIFE AND REIGN

TIM EWART

ANDRE
DEUTSCH

"Since her coronation in 1953, my grandmother The Queen has devoted her

life to the service of the public, leaving an extraordinary legacy that I, and the

rest of my family, are fortunate to inherit and learn from. The world has changed

dramatically over the course of The Queen's reign, and yet my grandmother

continues to inspire those of all generations with her sustained commitment to

the people of the UK and Commonwealth. These pages serve as a reminder of

The Queen's long and ongoing contribution to public life."

HRH The Duke of Cambridge

THIS IS AN ANDRE DEUTSCH BOOK

This updated edition published in 2018 by André Deutsch
An imprint of the Carlton Publishing Group
20 Mortimer Street
London W1T 3JW

First edition published in 2012 as *The Treasures of Queen Elizabeth*

Text © Tim Ewart 2012, 2016, 2018
Design © Carlton Publishing Group 2012, 2016

Printed in Dubai

A CIP catalogue for this book is available from the British Library

ISBN: 978 0 233 00555 3

10 9 8 7 6 5 4 3 2 1

Contents

INTRODUCTION 4

1 THE BIRTH OF A PRINCESS 6

2 LOVE AND WAR 16

3 THE ACCESSION 26

4 THE COMMONWEALTH 36

5 ROYAL DUTIES 46

6 THE QUEEN'S YEAR 56

7 PUBLIC PERCEPTIONS 66

8 GOOD YEARS AND BAD 76

9 THE GOLDEN YEARS 86

10 A DIAMOND JUBILEE 96

11 AN EXPANDING FAMILY 106

12 LONG TO REIGN OVER US 116

INDEX 126

CREDITS 128

RIGHT The young Princesses Elizabeth and
Margaret, aged just six and two. 12 August 1932.

Introduction

The sixth of February is my birthday, and in 1952 I turned three. My mother took me to stay in London as a special treat, and although my memory may be coloured by all I have read and seen since, I'm sure I can remember the crowds gathering outside Buckingham Palace and the salute of artillery guns to mark the death of King George VI. The following year, I watched on our black-and-white television as the Queen was crowned before I joined other children on the village green to celebrate with egg-and-spoon races and fancy dress contests. I went as Robin Hood.

The majority of people who live in Britain today simply can't remember a time when the Queen was not on the throne. She is part of our DNA. I believe it is important that those of us who report on the royal family remember that not everyone in Britain is an enthusiastic monarchist. But over six decades, through good times and bad, through controversy as well as moments of national celebration, the Queen has retained an extraordinary degree of public affection. No British monarch has reigned, or lived for so long. Only one other, the Queen's great-great grandmother Victoria, has reached a Diamond Jubilee.

When Elizabeth was born, Britain was recovering from one world war and the second was still 13 years away. She was 25 when she became Queen and her early overseas tours were made by ocean liner. Her first Christmas message was broadcast on the radio and it was another five years before she was seen live on television and extolling the benefits of "new technology". Now, the monarchy is on Facebook and has a Flickr account for its own photo stream.

This, then, is a record of Britain's second Elizabethan age, the story of a monarch who has witnessed social change which was unimaginable on that February day when she was told of her father's premature death and her own accession to the throne. It is a story told in pictures as well as words, pictures that record the major moments in Elizabeth's life and her reign. There are also reproduced documents printed on the page, which will bring the reader even closer to the extraordinary history of Queen Elizabeth II.

Tim Ewart

OPPOSITE The Queen on a visit to Tate & Lyle in March 2008 to celebrate 130 years of production by the company.

The Birth of a Princess

THE FIVE-STOREY HOUSE THAT ONCE STOOD AT NUMBER 17 BRUTON STREET IN THE EXCLUSIVE MAYFAIR AREA OF LONDON WAS DEMOLISHED YEARS AGO TO MAKE WAY FOR COMMERCIAL DEVELOPMENT. IT WAS FORMERLY THE HOME OF CLAUDE GEORGE BOWES-LYON, 14TH EARL OF STRATHMORE AND KINGHORNE, AND IT WAS THERE, IN THE EARLY HOURS OF 21 APRIL 1926, THAT HIS DAUGHTER, THE DUCHESS OF YORK, GAVE BIRTH TO HER FIRST CHILD. THE BABY'S NAME WAS ELIZABETH ALEXANDRA MARY, AND A QUARTER OF A CENTURY LATER SHE WAS TO BECOME QUEEN.

Today, a royal birth would see Bruton Street packed with television cameras and satellite trucks. The whole world would be watching. But in 1926 radio was still in its infancy and television broadcasts were several years away. News of Princess Elizabeth's birth was confined to a brief statement from Buckingham Palace: "The Duchess of York was safely delivered of a Princess at 2.40 this morning. Both mother and daughter are doing well." It was tucked away on page 14 of *The Times*. Nevertheless, crowds of well-wishers gathered on Bruton Street, and in the Coach and Horses pub on the corner, which still stands after re-building in the 1930s, glasses were raised in celebration.

Elizabeth's paternal grandparents, King George V and Queen Mary, were among the first visitors. Queen Mary wrote in her diary that the Princess was "a little darling with lovely complexion and pretty fair hair". The baby Elizabeth was now third in line to the throne, but she was not born to be Queen. Her father, the Duke of York, known in the family as Bertie, was the younger brother of Edward, Prince of Wales. Edward (known in the family as David) was unmarried, but the children it was assumed he would eventually have would come before Elizabeth in the order of succession, as would any of her own brothers. History, of course, was to take a dramatic turn.

Elizabeth was born into a life of privilege, but her parents were determined that any royal excess should be kept in check as she grew up. Britain was still recovering from the agony of the Great War of 1914–18

LEFT The Duke and Duchess of York, later King George VI and Queen Elizabeth, with Princess Elizabeth on her christening day in May 1926.

BELOW A first royal wave: the future Queen Elizabeth II as a toddler, greeting admirers from her pram.

RIGHT Princess Elizabeth at the age of seven, a portrait in oils by the Hungarian painter Philip de László, commissioned by her parents. De László was possibly chosen as he had already painted a portrait of the Duchess of York, the year before the Princess was born.

and society was changing. The old order was increasingly challenged, including the existence of the monarchy itself, and there was widespread industrial unrest that led to a general strike just days after Princess Elizabeth was born. King George V was acutely aware that the monarchy would remain aloof and out of touch at its peril. In one celebrated exchange with Lord Durham, a wealthy coal baron, he said of the miners, "You try living on their wages."

Elizabeth lived with her parents in Bruton Street until they moved into the family home, an imposing property nearby at 145 Piccadilly.

For all the intentions of a modest lifestyle, there was a retinue of servants to tend to the young Princess. Most important amongst them was Clara Knight, known as "Alla", the royal nursemaid, who cared for the Princess as she had her mother before her. Alla was cast in the mould of the classic British nanny, firm but loving. She stuck rigidly to a one-toy-at-a-time rule and was to shape the future Queen's formative years.

Royal tours now seldom last longer than a week or ten days, but things were very different then. Elizabeth was just nine months old when her parents set off on a journey by ocean liner through the Panama Canal to Fiji and on to New Zealand and Australia. They were away for six months. The new Princess may not have been with them, but she was certainly an object of intense interest. Australian newspapers nicknamed her "Betty" and the Duke and Duchess were given gifts for her at almost every event they attended and were bombarded with questions about her. The Duke wrote to his mother, "Where ever we go cheers are given for her as well and children write to us about her." By the time the tour

1

PROGRAMME

OF

Christmas Pantomime
ALADDIN

IN THE

WATERLOO CHAMBER
WINDSOR CASTLE

DECEMBER 16th, 17th and 18th, 1943

PRICE 1s.

2

was over, an estimated three tons of presents had been collected for Elizabeth.

If the Princess missed her parents, there is little evidence of it. Her routine with Alla continued uninterrupted, including long outings in her pram through the royal parks of central London. But Alla was not her only companion. King George and Queen Mary had no hesitation in playing the role of doting grandparents. The Queen called her "the bambino". Elizabeth developed a particularly close relationship with her grandfather the King in those early years. As

BELOW AND OPPOSITE A scrapbook of images of moments in the Queen's childhood, which are as follows:

1. A charming photograph of the Queen as a baby being carried up the steps of Balmoral in her perambulator in 1927.

2. The programme that was printed for the performance of the pantomime Aladdin that Princesses Elizabeth and Margaret Rose performed

at Windsor Castle on 15 December 1943. The money raised from the sale of tickets was used to buy wool to knit socks for the armed forces.

3. An image of the production of Aladdin Princesses Elizabeth and Margaret Rose can be seen on the far right of the photograph.

4. Princess Elizabeth takes part in a swimming contest at the Bath Club in Piccadilly in London on 29 June 1939.

3

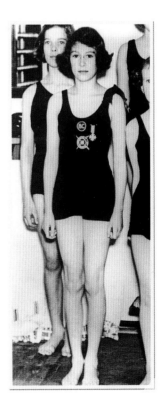

4

she found her voice, she referred to herself as "Tillibet", later to become "Lillibet", and to him as "Grandpa England". The Archbishop of Canterbury found them at play one day, the King on all fours as a horse with the Princess leading him by the beard. And all this with a monarch who was better known for his gruff ill temper. On her fourth birthday in 1930, George V gave the future Elizabeth II a Shetland pony called Peggy and her lifelong love of horses began.

Exactly four months later, Elizabeth had a sister. Margaret Rose was born at Glamis Castle in Scotland, the country seat of the Earl of Strathmore. The family that the Duke of York was to refer to as "us four" was complete. A close-knit, loving family it was too. Elizabeth and Margaret Rose undoubtedly fought, but they remained devoted to each other until Princess Margaret's death in 2002. Within two years of Margaret Rose's arrival there was another new and influential nanny on the scene: Marion Crawford, known as "Crawfie". It is from her book, *The Little Princesses*, published many years later over the objections of the royal family, that many of our perceptions of Princess Elizabeth's early years are based. She was seen as the more serious and responsible of the two sisters, while Margaret Rose was mischievous. Winston Churchill supported the view. When Elizabeth was just two he wrote of her: "She has an air of authority and reflectiveness astonishing in an infant."

Those early years were a wonderful and happy time for Princess Elizabeth and her sister. They were educated at home under the direction of Crawfie, who wrote: "The Duke and Duchess, most happy in their own married life, were not over concerned with the higher education of their daughters. They wanted most for them a really happy childhood." But huge change lay ahead.

The Duke of York fulfilled his royal duties conscientiously, but he was not comfortable in the public gaze. Bertie had endured a difficult childhood, not least at the hands of nannies who had shown little of the kindness that Alla and Crawfie showered on his own children. The result was ill health and a stammer, now immortalized in the film *The King's Speech*. The Australian-born therapist Lionel Logue helped greatly, but Bertie never lost his aversion to public speaking. The last thing he would want was to be King.

George V died on 20 January 1936, and the crown passed to Edward, a very different character to the shy and hesitant Duke of York. Edward VIII was handsome, assured and at ease in any company, a popular figure who enjoyed the limelight. The problem was the woman at his side: the American divorcée and socialite Wallis Simpson. The rest of the royal family disliked her and she was simply unacceptable to the establishment of the day as a future queen. Such was the aversion to divorcées at the time that they were banned from the royal box at Ascot.

The events of 1936 were traumatic for the Duke and Duchess of York, although it's certain that their two daughters were shielded as much as possible from the controversy that raged around them. The King was determined

OPPOSITE An eight-year-old Princess Elizabeth with her grandparents, King George V and Queen Mary, on their way to Westminster Abbey for a service in 1934.

BELOW Friends together: Princess Elizabeth (third from right) and Princess Margaret (second from left) at a birthday party for the young Master of Carnegie in September 1935.

THE DAILY MIRROR, Friday, December 11, 1936.

Daily Mirror

No. 10306   Registered at the G.P.O. as a newspaper.   ONE PENNY

LONDON ED.

KING EDWARD WILL BROADCAST TO-NIGHT

Edward VIII, immediately he signs the abdication papers to-night, will broadcast to the Empire "as a private person owing allegiance to the new King." The broadcast has tentatively been fixed for 10 p.m.

The British Empire yesterday received with utmost calm the announcement of the abdication. It welcomed with affection the accession of the Duke and Duchess of York.

The new King dined with his brother last night at Fort Belvedere.

The King's last message: Page 2; A toast "Across the Water": Page 3; Mr. Baldwin's revelations: Pages 4 and 5; Love ended a reign: Page 6; What the world thinks: Page 7.

FLAG DROPS AS THE KING SIGNS

King Edward signed the Instrument of Abdication at 10 a.m. yesterday in his study on the ground floor of Fort Belvedere.

He signed in the presence of the Duke of York, the Duke of Kent and the Duke of Gloucester.

As the documents were signed, the flag of the Duchy of Cornwall, which has been flying over Fort Belvedere since his Majesty's arrival, was lowered. Later, it was run up again.

The Act of Abdication will be taken to the King to sign at Fort Belvedere to-night.

RIGHT AND OPPOSITE The front page of the *Daily Mirror* from the day of King Edward VIII's abdication on 11 December 1936, and one of the inside pages from the same edition with a feature article entitled "The Story of the Great Little Sisters".

12

Friday, December 11, 1936   THE DAILY MIRROR   Page 15

The story of the great

LITTLE SISTERS

> All the world talks of two little sisters to-day.
> Princess Elizabeth, aged ten, and Princess Margaret Rose, aged six.
> Ever since the royal children were born,
>
> **CYRIL JAMES**
>
> has kept a scrap-book of their doings and sayings.
> He has dipped into that record to write this intriguing year-by-year story of the two great little sisters.

IN THE BEGINNING

WHISPERING crowds collect on the pavements of Bruton-street. Eyes gaze at the discreet door of a stately home—number seventeen.

"Yes, my dear, to-night, they think."

"I remember the Duchess coming out of that door on her wedding day. Three years ago—doesn't time fly? A lovely bride. I always said she was the prettiest ever."

Big cars purr to a standstill outside the house. A little man with a puckered face alights and runs up the steps.

The Home Secretary. "It's Jix, Sir William Joynson-Hicks. Yes, he always has to be present when . . ."

The news spreads from the house with the lighted windows to the waiting crowd.

A daughter is born to the Duchess of York.
A lovely daughter.
And the date is April 23, 1926.

THE FIRST YEAR

"But what a good baby." They all make the same comment.

To the cradleside comes Queen Mary. As she looks down upon the sleeping child her face is filled with the mellow sweetness of memory.

"I do wish," says the Queen with a smile, "you were more like your little mother."

Three months pass. The child is taken to Glamis. In grim, grey, ghostly Glamis Castle a baby smiles and crows.

THE SECOND YEAR

Around the nursery crawls little Elizabeth Alexandra Mary. With a rather stylish crawl. She sits upright, and, using one leg as an "oar," pushes herself around the room.

Mummy and Daddy are away in Australia. But there is always Grandmother, with her welcoming cry of "Bambino!"

Suddenly Mummy is back.

Elizabeth greets her with her first word.

"Mummy! Mummy!"

And she is learning to walk. "A dangerous business," writes the Duchess to a friend.

THE THIRD YEAR

Sad faces all around the baby. Her prattle strikes across the hushed voices.

Grandpa is ill. Grandpa is very ill.

And now Grandpa is well again. His eyes twinkle as he listens to her chatter. The doctors know that here is physic more potent than any they have devised.

Elizabeth sits on the knee of George V.

The Duke and Duchess of York buy a large brown toy Shetland pony and take it back to Elizabeth.

"I want Elizabeth to be a good horsewoman when she grows up," says the Duke, "and she will soon be able to start riding lessons in play, at any rate."

THE FOURTH YEAR

Dialogue in the nursery.

"Now, you must learn to curtsy when you meet your grandparents. They are King and Queen."

"I can't curtsey!"

Later the King enters the room.

Elizabeth makes a low curtsy—with her back to George V.

"There, Danpa, I have curtsied."

The King smiles and gathers her up in his arms.

THE FIFTH YEAR

Elizabeth walks in the sunshine at the back of Buckingham Palace. There is a click of heels, a flash of steel as a sentry presents arms.

The little girl looks at the soldier and laughs. She passes him, turns back and passes again.

Once more the sentry stands rigidly presenting arms.

Again and again this happens, until the soldier's face is as scarlet as his tunic.

A horrified officer appears, summons Elizabeth's nurse. The child is taken away from the exhausted sentry.

And later—a great event.

For at Glamis is born a baby sister, Princess Margaret Rose.

THE SIXTH YEAR

Tiny hands are busy with needle and thread. Elizabeth has learned to sew, and is making a dress for her 3ft. doll, Julie.

The Princess sneezes. She has a cold.

"Off to bed."

"Then Julie has a cold, too."

So to bed Julie must go as well.

Baby Margaret Rose stares wonderingly at this strange new world.

"Mum," says Margaret Rose—her first word.

"Dad," she manages a little later.

And then—to Elizabeth's unspeakable delight, the baby learns her third word.

"Sis."

As Elizabeth makes a prim little bow to onlookers who watch her, the baby bobs forward, too.

THE SEVENTH YEAR

Soliloquy by the Princess.

"Oh, this growing-up isn't all fun. Now they're putting a whole extra hour on lessons in the morning. AND in the afternoon. It wouldn't be so bad if I only had to learn

The whole world worships them to-day

French from that gramophone thing. Or dancing.

"Ooh, yes—and singing lessons all day.

"Oh, Margaret Rose, wait until you grow up."

THE EIGHTH YEAR

Elizabeth's first Royal Garden Party. She is nervous, but tries to assume Grandmother's air as she steps from a car. She is wearing a frilly pink muslin dress. Then——

"Whooooooooosh."

The wind plucks the hat from her golden head. She looks after it sadly. Then consoles herself with a slice of bread-and-butter.

Christmas comes. Two little figures in cherry-red, Elizabeth and Margaret Rose, are with their mother at the Albert Hall. Their clear voices are lost in a rush of sound:

"Oh come, all ye faithful,
Joyful and triumphant."

Elizabeth looks gravely at Mr. Ramsay MacDonald.

"I often see your picture in the papers."

Ramsay smiles.

"Yes, the other day I saw one of you leading a flock of geese!"

Elizabeth and Margaret Rose are at the circus.

"Ooooh!" the sisters exclaim together as an acrobat flies from one trapeze to another.

Then a clown, a grotesque figure in comical costume, dead-white face and blood-red lips, approaches the Royal Box.

Princess Margaret Rose shrinks back timidly.

"No . . . no . . . a clown. . . ."

Elizabeth shakes hands boldly and encourages her sister.

Timidly, Margaret Rose extends a tiny hand.

THE NINTH YEAR

Elizabeth gets out of bed at Royal Lodge, Windsor Park.

The blinds are drawn. Somewhere a bell is tolling, tolling, tolling.

They tell her why everyone has been so sad, so anxious.

Grandfather is dead.

Grandfather, who had laughed and joked at Sandringham, Balmoral, Windsor. Grandfather, who, in his busiest moments, always had a smile and a gentle word for the two sisters.

The bells toll on.

THE TENTH YEAR

In the garden of their Piccadilly home, Elizabeth and Margaret Rose are playing.

Elizabeth is riding her bicycle along the drive.

Margaret Rose steps on the path and holds up one chubby hand.

And Margaret solemnly trots across the path.

"Oh, yes, that's our newest game—pedestrians' crossings."

Princess Elizabeth speaks.

"I want to buy that tin of toffee."

"Certainly, your Royal Highness."

Princess Margaret Rose speaks.

"I want that woolly duck."

Elizabeth takes her own money from her own handbag, and, at a Scottish sale of work, gravely pays for both.

And, hand in hand, the little Princesses pass the decorated stalls.

Growing up . . . growing to sweet and gracious girlhood.

to marry Mrs Simpson, but it quickly became apparent that he could not keep her and the throne. On 7 December he told his brother that he intended to abdicate, and Bertie sobbed openly in his mother's arms. Four days later Edward announced to the nation in a radio broadcast: "I have found it impossible to carry the heavy burden of responsibility and to discharge my duties as king as I would wish to do without the help and support of the woman I love." The Duke of York was now the reluctant King George VI.

Princess Elizabeth's life was to change forever. The serious little girl who liked nothing better than her ponies and dogs, who was so happy with family life, was now the ten-year-old heiress presumptive to the throne. She spent that Christmas at Sandringham. Her grandmother, Queen Mary, rarely left her room; her mother had influenza, and her father was still trying to come to terms with the task he now faced. "Us four" were at their lowest ebb.

Within two months the family moved to Buckingham Palace. Princess Elizabeth was tutored in constitutional history to prepare her for the role that lay ahead. While she studied and her sister Margaret Rose explored the corridors of their new home on a tricycle, the armies of Europe began to stir for the second time in the twentieth century as the world prepared again for war.

OPPOSITE King George VI after his coronation in May 1937, with his wife Queen Elizabeth and the two Princesses.

ABOVE A day at the zoo: the young Princesses clearly enjoying an elephant ride at London Zoo in May 1939, accompanied by their governess and some friends.

RIGHT Royal souvenir: a commemorative postcard issued to celebrate the coronation of George VI.

CROWNED at Westminster Abbey 12th May 1937

PRINCESS ELIZABETH PRINCESS MARGARET ROSE

SOUVENIR of the CORONATION of THEIR MAJESTIES KING GEORGE VI & QUEEN ELIZABETH

Love and War

IN JULY 1939, JUST WEEKS BEFORE THE OUTBREAK OF THE
SECOND WORLD WAR, 13-YEAR-OLD PRINCESS ELIZABETH
ACCOMPANIED HER PARENTS ON A TOUR OF THE ROYAL NAVAL
COLLEGE AT DARTMOUTH. IT WAS TO PROVE A TURNING POINT
IN HER LIFE. AMONG THE CADETS ON HAND TO ESCORT THE
ROYAL PARTY WAS PRINCE PHILIP OF GREECE AND DENMARK,
18 YEARS OLD, SPIRITED AND HANDSOME.

Elizabeth and Philip were distant cousins and had met before at various family gatherings, but this time it was different as Philip joined Elizabeth and her sister Margaret for tea and ginger biscuits. Lord Louis Mountbatten, the King's cousin and Philip's uncle, observed in his diary that "tea was a great success with the children". It was a masterful understatement. Elizabeth had fallen in love.

There was, of course, to be no whirlwind romance. On 3 September the British Prime Minister Neville Chamberlain announced on BBC radio that "this nation is at war with Germany". Prince Philip, now a midshipman in the Royal Navy, was soon in action. His wartime service took him from the Indian Ocean to the Mediterranean, the North Sea and the Pacific. He was mentioned in despatches for his service in the Battle of Matapan off the coast of Crete in 1941 and was awarded the Greek War Cross for Valour.

The royal family could not, naturally, influence the course of the war, but they played a crucial role. The King and Queen were portrayed as embodying the spirit of British fortitude in facing the threat posed by the enemy. In 1940 Buckingham Palace suffered a direct hit from a German bomber, prompting Queen Elizabeth to remark that "now we can look the East End in the face". Her visits to London's East End, an area that was suffering grievously in the Blitz, provided some of the most enduring images of the wartime city and did much to raise morale. At Buckingham Palace, America's visiting First Lady, Eleanor Roosevelt, was startled to find a line round the inside of her bath limiting the amount of water she should use. It was said that the King had done it himself.

BELOW A 14-year-old Princess Elizabeth, with Princess Margaret, makes her wartime *Children's Hour* broadcast from Buckingham Palace, 1940.

A few weeks after the palace bomb, Princess Elizabeth made the first of many royal broadcasts. Her wartime address to the nation was an indication of how serious the situation was perceived to be in that early phase of the war. The palace had previously refused attempts to put the Princess on the air, most notably by the United States, where she had been invited to broadcast two years earlier to mark National Children's Week. Palace officials made it clear

that the Princess would do no such thing "for several years to come".

But now, on 13 October 1940, with Britain facing its darkest hour, the day's edition of the enormously popular *Children's Hour* was preceded by an announcer. In the clipped tones of the day he declared, "This is the BBC Home Service. Hello children everywhere. This is one of the most important days in the history of *Children's Hour*." Princess Elizabeth was to

BELOW An original draft of the speech that the 14-year-old Princess Elizabeth made to children in Britain and throughout the Commonwealth on 13 October 1939. Her sister, Princess Margaret Rose was with her when Elizabeth made the speech – the first time she had been heard in public – and together they wished listeners good night. The recording was such a success that it was later issued as a gramophone record.

Draft of Speech for the Princess Elizabeth.

Now, I want to talk to all the little boys and girls who are listening in. And I want to say just this to you - there's nothing at all to be frightened about. You're all going away for a lovely holiday.

I want you all to be very good and to do just as you're told and take great care of your gas masks. I've got one, too, I've just been trying it on and I looked so funny in it that Rose laughed and laughed until she nearly cried ! Now, you will do as I ask you won't you ? Do just as you're told and take care of your gas masks !

Oh, and there's just one thing more, I'm going away, too ! But, I've made Daddy promise that he'll let me travel all over the country and come and visit you all. Because, dear Children, I am a Princess of England, and one day - I hope it will be far, far away - I may be your Queen and I always remember that great Queen Elizabeth and how she lived for her People and I'm going to do my best to follow her example and live for you. And so my dear, dear Children, Goodbye, until I see you!

address "children of the Empire at home and overseas". The broadcast can still be played in full on the royal family's official website and it is a fascinating piece of history since it was the first time the future Queen was heard in public.

The message was one of optimism, a rallying cry to keep the faith, to believe that good would triumph over evil. "I can truthfully say to you all that we children at home are full of cheerfulness and courage," said the Princess. And she concluded: "We know, every one of us, that in the end all will be well; for God will care for us

and give us victory and peace. And when peace comes, remember it will be for us, the children of today, to make the world of tomorrow a better and happier place."

Princess Margaret, still only ten years old, was at her sister's side in the studio. "My sister and I are going to say goodnight to you," declared Elizabeth. "Come on, Margaret." And together they wished their listeners goodnight and good luck. The effect was immediate and far-reaching. In the United States, where admiration for the royal family had been tempered by support for

ABOVE Princess Elizabeth and her parents in April 1944, just before her eighteenth birthday.

OPPOSITE The wartime Princess: Elizabeth as a second subaltern in the Auxiliary Territorial Service, 1945.

the former King Edward VIII and Mrs Simpson, there were repeated calls for the broadcast to be aired again. Officials at Buckingham Palace, quick to seize the moment, turned the broadcast into a gramophone record for sale in America and across the British Empire.

The Princesses did not stay at Buckingham Palace during the war. Like so many children in London, they became evacuees. Unlike the others, they were not, of course, sent to live with families in Wales or rural areas deemed safe from German bombs, but to the royal residences of Sandringham, Balmoral and Windsor Castle. There had been a suggestion that Elizabeth and Margaret should be sent to Canada, but the Queen retorted, "The children won't go without me. I won't leave without the King. And the King will never leave."

Elizabeth did her bit for the war effort. She and her sister put on pantomimes at Windsor Castle to raise money for the Queen's Wool

ABOVE RIGHT The look of love: Prince Philip of Greece and Princess Elizabeth, now 20, at a family wedding in 1946.

RIGHT Princesses Elizabeth (left) and Margaret (right) enjoying deck games on HMS *Vanguard* while travelling to South Africa for the royal tour in 1947.

OPPOSITE Princess Elizabeth performing one of her earliest royal duties, launching the aircraft carrier HMS *Eagle* in Belfast, 1946.

Fund, which bought the material for military uniforms. Elizabeth was a Girl Guide and later joined the Women's Auxiliary Territorial Service, training as a driver and mechanic. And throughout the war a steady stream of photographs of the two Princesses was used to bolster the propaganda effort. They were the symbol of a British way of life being defended against Nazi tyranny.

However much Elizabeth may or may not have known about the progress of the war, her father was very much in the loop. The King had not always seen eye to eye with Winston Churchill, and found Churchill's predecessor Neville Chamberlain an easier man to get along with. The relationship was not helped by Churchill's initial support for Edward VIII during the abdication crisis. But as the war dragged on, things changed. The King was regularly briefed by Churchill on the details of British campaigns, and was one of only a handful of senior figures to be kept abreast of exactly how badly or how well things were going.

When victory was secured in 1945, Churchill joined King George VI and Queen Elizabeth on the balcony at Buckingham Palace to wave to the thousands who packed the Mall to celebrate. And amongst that crowd, anonymous and unnoticed, enjoying a rare moment of freedom, was the heiress to the throne. The idea had, inevitably, been Princess Margaret's. She alone among a group of young people who had been at a palace dinner was out of uniform. The Princesses sang and cheered with everyone else and even stole a sailor's cap.

Prince Philip of Greece had exchanged letters with Princess Elizabeth throughout the war and in 1943 had been a guest at one of her Windsor Castle fund-raising pantomimes. Their courtship began when the war came to an end, although many in the British establishment were uneasy about Philip's German family connections (the Greek royal family was of Danish-German origin; its surname was Schleswig-Holstein-Sonderburg-Glücksburg). Early in 1947 the King and Queen embarked

on a tour of South Africa, taking with them both of the young Princesses. Many saw it as a way of giving Elizabeth a chance to make up her mind about marrying Philip. There was certainly ample time for reflection, as the royal family was away for four months. If there were any doubts, they were soon dispelled. On 9 July 1947, the engagement was announced between HRH Princess Elizabeth and Lieutenant Philip Mountbatten, who had changed his family name to that of his British maternal grandparents. Elizabeth had already

started performing royal duties in her own right and Philip accompanied her on her last such engagement as a single woman, launching the ocean liner *Caronia* on the River Clyde.

They married the same year, on 20 November, at Westminster Abbey. The build-up to a royal wedding was attended by feverish media interest (as it would be again 64 years later, for their grandson's marriage in 2011). The cake, the presents and, most particularly, the dress were the subjects of endless debate and speculation. In post-war

Norman Hartnell.

LEFT The design for
Princess Elizabeth's
wedding dress by Sir
Norman Hartnell,
which shows the
degree of embroidery
detail that was to be
included in the dress.
Sir Norman had begun
creating designs for
members of the royal
family in 1935 and he
went on to design the
dress worn by Queen
Elizabeth for her
coronation in 1953.

OPPOSITE A plan of
Westminster Abbey
and the surrounding
area showing details
of the arrangements
that were made
for the wedding of
Princess Elizabeth
with Prince Philip,
Duke of Edinburgh.

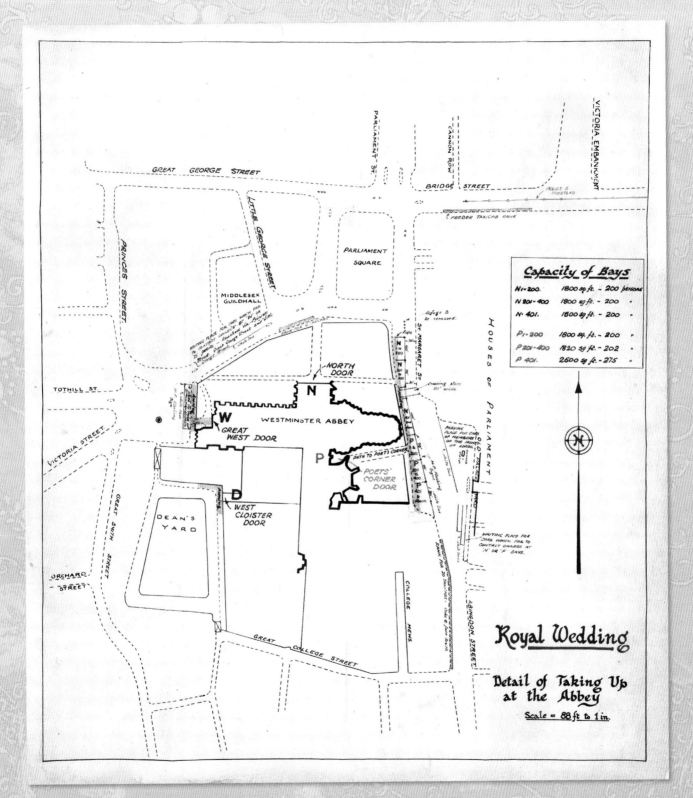

Capacity of Bays

N 1-200.	1800 sq ft.	200 persons
N 201-400	1800 sq ft.	200 "
N 401.	1800 sq ft.	200 "
P 1-200.	1800 sq ft.	200 "
P 201-400.	1820 sq ft.	202 "
P 401.	2500 sq ft.	275 "

Royal Wedding

Detail of Taking Up
at the Abbey

Scale = 88 ft. to 1 in.

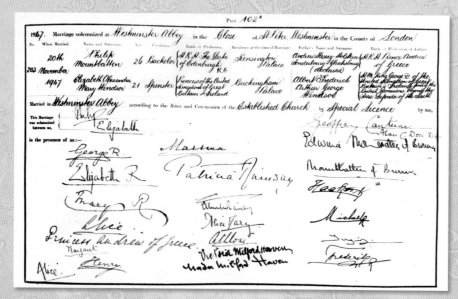

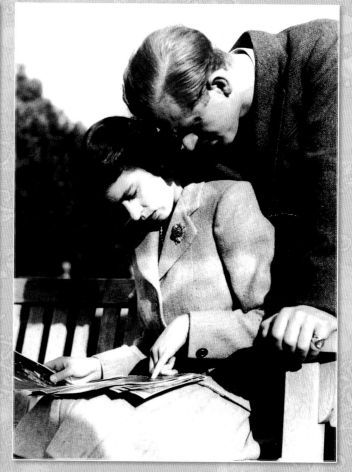

LEFT The marriage certificate of Princess Elizabeth and the Duke of Edinburgh which contains the signatures of King George VI and Queen Elizabeth as well as Princess Margaret and other witnesses.

BELOW LEFT Wedding day: huge crowds line the streets to greet Princess Elizabeth and Prince Philip on 20 November 1947.

BELOW The royal newlyweds on their honeymoon in Romsey, Hampshire.

OPPOSITE Smile please: the official wedding photograph of Elizabeth and Philip.

Britain, with its continuing rationing and mood of austerity, how extravagant should such an occasion be? Should the royal family reflect the economic constraints felt by their subjects, or should parsimony be thrown to the winds and everyone be encouraged to celebrate a royal spectacular?

In the event, in spite of sugar rationing, there were 12 wedding cakes – one four feet high – and nearly 2,500 presents from around the world. The wedding dress, designed by Norman Hartnell, was made of ivory satin and decorated with 10,000 white pearls imported from America. It cost 300 clothing coupons and an additional £1,200, the equivalent of about £37,000 in today's money.

The wedding itself was a grand, glittering event, broadcast live on radio to 42 countries. It was filmed and shown that evening on BBC television and later around the world. The 2,000 invitations were highly prized and many would-be guests were disappointed. Members of Parliament, for example, had to enter a ballot to secure a place. But there was no shortage of foreign royalty. The Abbey's pews were packed with the crowned heads of Europe and their families, some already exiles from their own lands. They heard Princess Elizabeth exchange vows with the man who now bore the title His Royal Highness The Duke of Edinburgh. The couple were driven back to Buckingham Palace through cheering crowds to join 150 guests at a wedding breakfast. The King made a toast, although not a speech, and later the newlyweds were showered with rose petals and cheered by waiting crowds as they were driven in a horse-drawn carriage to Waterloo Station to begin a very British honeymoon.

Britain had shrugged off its economic gloom and celebrated the wedding with enthusiasm. The royal family had emerged from the war with its reputation and its standing enhanced. Memories of the abdication crisis had been banished, and at home and abroad the monarchy had seldom enjoyed greater popularity. But the crown was soon to pass to a new generation.

The Accession

LESS THAN SIX YEARS LATER, IN 1953, WESTMINSTER ABBEY SAW PRINCESS ELIZABETH AT THE CENTRE OF AN EVEN GRANDER, MORE ELABORATE CEREMONY THAN HER WEDDING – HER CORONATION. THE INTERVENING YEARS OFFERED HER, HOWEVER BRIEFLY, THE GLIMPSE OF A LIFE AS NORMAL AND AS UNENCUMBERED WITH FORMALITY AS ANY SENIOR MEMBER OF THE ROYAL FAMILY COULD HOPE TO ENJOY. BUT IT ENDED PREMATURELY.

Elizabeth and Philip did not wait to start a family. Their first son, Charles Philip Arthur George, was born at Buckingham Palace just after nine o'clock in the evening on 14 November 1948, six days before his parents' first wedding anniversary. Prince Philip was playing squash at the time and was hastily summoned to his wife's bedside. Crowds gathered outside the palace, the fountains in Trafalgar Square were dyed blue in Charles's honour and Princess Elizabeth declared that food parcels should be sent to the mothers of every other child born in Britain on that day.

Delighted as she was with her first son – and she wrote glowingly about him to friends – Princess Elizabeth was separated from Charles for prolonged periods in his early life. His first two Christmases were spent away from his parents. Like his mother, he was left during those months of separation in the care of his grandparents, King George and Queen Elizabeth, at Sandringham, and he remained deeply attached to his grandmother, soon to become Queen Mother, until her death in 2002 at the age of 101.

Prince Philip was still a serving officer in the Royal Navy, a job he loved, and when a posting presented itself on the island of Malta, he seized the opportunity. It was the autumn of 1949 and Philip was made second in command of the destroyer HMS *Chequers* in the Mediterranean fleet. Within a month, he was joined in Malta by the Princess, but not their son. Home was the Villa Guardamangia, rented by Philip's uncle Lord Mountbatten. The months she spent in Malta offered the Princess the carefree lifestyle of a navy wife. She drove herself, went shopping for herself and savoured the sun. And she became pregnant for a second time.

Princess Anne Elizabeth Alice Louise was born at Clarence House, close to Buckingham Palace, on 15 August 1950. Prince Philip came back to London for the occasion but returned to Malta barely two weeks later. Elizabeth joined him in December, now leaving two children with the King and Queen for Christmas. Philip was promoted to his first naval command, aboard the frigate HMS *Magpie*, and for a few more months, life continued as before in Malta.

There was, however, a cloud above Elizabeth's Mediterranean idyll. The health of her father had been deteriorating alarmingly, and by 1951 it was apparent that the King

RIGHT King George VI (left) and Queen Elizabeth (right) with the proud parents at the christening of Prince Charles at Buckingham Palace, 1948.

BELOW Happy family: Elizabeth and Philip with their children Charles and Anne in 1951. This is the first colour photograph of Princess Anne.

RIGHT The new Queen Elizabeth II returns to England from Africa in February 1952 after the death of her father, George VI.

needed support in his official duties. That summer, Elizabeth and Philip flew home from Malta for the last time. In September, the King underwent a three-hour operation to remove his left lung. The operation was deemed a success, but the signs were ominous. Winston Churchill, soon to be re-elected Prime Minister, was warned by his own doctor that "even if the King recovers, he can scarcely live more than a year". Even that was an optimistic prediction.

For Elizabeth and Philip things had already changed dramatically. The young couple, who had appeared so relaxed in Malta and had so often been the life and soul of the party, were now very much on official duty. In October 1951, they became the first members of the royal family to fly across the Atlantic, taking over the King's postponed tour of Canada. It lasted more than a month, covered 10,000 miles and culminated with a visit to President Truman in the White House. Throughout the tour, Elizabeth's private secretary had carried with him the papers of accession that would be needed in the event of her father's death.

Barely two months after their return from Canada, the Princess and her husband were called on to take the King's place on another

BUCKINGHAM PALACE

November 14th 1948

The Princess Elizabeth, Duchess of Edinburgh was safely delivered of a Prince at nine fourteen pm today.

Her Royal Highness and her son are both doing well.

W. Gilliatt M.S. F.R.C.O.G.
John H Peel. Pres. F.R.C.O.G.
V.F.Hall FFA R.C.S D.A.
John Weir M.B.

state visit, this time to Australia and New Zealand, with a stop en route in Kenya. Elizabeth and Philip flew from Heathrow Airport on 31 January 1952, and the King went to bid them farewell. He lingered on the runway in a bitter wind until the aircraft was out of sight, and it was the last time he saw the daughter he loved so much.

King George VI died in his sleep at Sandringham early in the morning of 6 February. He was 56 years old and had been on the throne for 15 years. Elizabeth was watching and photographing game at Treetops Lodge in Kenya and it took some time for

ABOVE The announcement issued from Buckingham Palace on 14 November 1948 of the birth of Prince Charles. It is signed by the doctors who were in attendance.

confirmation of the King's death to reach the officials accompanying her. Eventually Prince Philip took her for a walk in the garden and broke the news to her.

The King was buried nine days later. After his coffin lay in state at Westminster Hall, his funeral service was held at St George's Chapel, Windsor Castle. Britain greatly mourned the King who had not wanted the crown, a man ill at ease in public, but a monarch who came to personify the spirit of wartime Britain. More than 300,000 people stood in line to see his body at Westminster Hall. But after grieving, the country prepared to celebrate the coronation of its new Queen.

Elizabeth was not crowned until 2 June the following year, a day chosen after lengthy consultations with meteorologists, who declared it the most likely date for good weather. They were wrong: it rained on the biggest royal parade modern Britain had ever seen, but neither the weather nor the recent death of the Queen's grandmother Queen Mary could dampen spirits. To add to the mood of celebration, news arrived on the same day that Edmund Hillary, the New Zealander who was part of a British expedition, had become the first person to reach the summit of Mount Everest.

If the crowds who camped out overnight along the procession route had been ill-prepared for that sodden coronation day, the Queen was not. Elizabeth was only 26 when she ascended the throne, but there were older and wiser heads to steer her through those intimidating first months as monarch. Foremost among them, of course, was Winston Churchill. Britain's great wartime leader spent six years in opposition until he was re-elected in 1951 at the age of 77. Now he became the new Queen's most enthusiastic ally, relishing their weekly audiences and helping to steer her through the bewildering affairs of state that suddenly confronted her.

Churchill was determined that the coronation would be a moment of grand

celebration in a nation still very much in the grip of post-war austerity – a moment of solemn dignity, but a party too. It was meticulously planned, but not without argument and controversy. The key area of debate? Television coverage. Fewer than two million people in Britain had television sets at the time, but the BBC believed that the coronation should be covered live. The Queen, Churchill and a legion of palace advisers were against it. There were fears about turning the coronation into a piece of theatre complete with intrusive close-ups of the monarch. But when permission was refused there was a public outcry, angry newspaper editorials and debates in Parliament. It was finally agreed that television cameras would be allowed in, although the anointment and Holy Communion could not be shown. It was a turning point in relations between the palace and a hitherto compliant media.

The coronation was, of course, the ultimate theatre: dignified and solemn, yes, but a breath-taking spectacle too. The Queen, with Prince Philip at her side, travelled to Westminster Abbey in the gold state coach drawn by eight grey horses. She wore a white satin dress designed by Norman Hartnell and embroidered with the emblems of the United Kingdom and the Commonwealth. It may have been live on television, but the ceremony itself had changed little over more than a thousand years. There have been coronations on the site of Westminster Abbey since the eleventh century, when Edward the Confessor built the first church. On Christmas Day in 1066, William the Conqueror was the first king to be crowned here. The coronation chair used by Elizabeth dated back to 1300 and the crown placed on her head had been re-made for the coronation of Charles II in 1661. The service began with Geoffrey Fisher, the Archbishop of Canterbury, asking, "Madam, is your Majesty willing to take the oath?" And the Queen replying, "I am

TOP First Christmas broadcast: the Queen at the microphone at Sandringham, December 1952.

ABOVE The coronation, on 2 June 1953. The Queen is wearing the St Edward Crown and holding the sceptre and the rod.

OPPOSITE Cecil Beaton's official coronation portrait photograph of Queen Elizabeth II, in full regalia.

willing." There was an act of homage from Prince Philip: "I do become your liege man of life and limb, and of earthly worship." And at the end, the congregation shouted, "God save Queen Elizabeth, long live Queen Elizabeth, may the Queen live for ever."

Elizabeth carried it off with remarkable poise. A young, almost diminutive princess in a sea of elderly bishops in all their finery became the Queen for a new age. Later, the royal family made no fewer than six appearances on the balcony of Buckingham Palace to satisfy an enormous, celebrating crowd. And in front rooms across the nation, on the streets, in parks and on village greens, Britain had its party.

It had, too, its new Elizabethan Age, although that appears to be a description the Queen herself has never much cared for. In a broadcast the following year, she observed, "Frankly I do not myself feel at all like my great Tudor forebear, who was blessed with neither husband nor children, who ruled as a despot and was never able to leave her native shores."

This Elizabeth was to leave her native shores as no monarch before her. She was to see an empire change to a commonwealth and as it did so she was to traverse the globe time and time again. Elizabeth was crowned in a black-and-white Britain, but she was to reign over a nation that would change in a way none of her forebears could possibly have imagined.

....

RIGHT The oath of allegiance signed by the Queen at her Coronation on 2 June 1953. More than 8000 guests attended the ceremony and some 20 million people watched the coverage of it on television. The broadcast was made in 44 languages. An estimated 3 million people lined the streets of London to catch a glimpse of the new Queen who travelled to and from Westminster Abbey in the gold State Coach.

I solemnly promise and swear to govern the Peoples of the United Kingdom of Great Britain and Northern Ireland, Canada, Australia, New Zealand and the Union of South Africa, Pakistan and Ceylon, and of my Possessions and the other Territories to any of them belonging or pertaining, according to their respective laws and customs.

I will to my power cause Law and Justice, in Mercy, to be executed in all my judgements.

I will to the utmost of my power maintain the Laws of God and the true profession of the Gospel. I will to the utmost of my power maintain in the United Kingdom the Protestant Reformed Religion established by law. And I will maintain and preserve inviolably the settlement of the Church of England, and the doctrine, worship, discipline, and government thereof, as by law established in England. And I will preserve unto the Bishops and Clergy of England, and to the Churches there committed to their charge, all such rights and privileges as by law do or shall appertain to them or any of them.

The things which I have here before promised, I will perform and keep.

So help me God.

FAR RIGHT The coronation procession passes through the huge crowds of people who had lined the route on the way back to Buckingham Palace,. It was a colourful spectacle despite looming grey skies and glistening-wet streets.

RIGHT AND BELOW Emblems of sovereignty: St Edward's Crown and the orb. Like the crown, the orb dates from 1661.

BELOW The royal family on the balcony at Buckingham Palace after the coronation. Apparently a little overwhelmed, Prince Charles and Princess Anne attempt a wave.

An extract of pages from the special Coronation edition of the *Illustrated London News* from June 1953. The pages featured artists' sketches of some of the more solemn moments of the Coronation ceremony as well as photographs of members of the royal family and others who were involved in the occasion.

The Commonwealth

DURING THE REIGN OF THE QUEEN'S GRANDFATHER, KING GEORGE V, BRITANNIA QUITE LITERALLY RULED THE WAVES. BY 1922, THE BRITISH EMPIRE COVERED ALMOST A QUARTER OF THE WORLD'S LAND MASS AND CONTAINED A QUARTER OF ITS POPULATION. GEORGE WAS NOT JUST KING; HE WAS KING-EMPEROR. BY THE TIME OF THE QUEEN'S DIAMOND JUBILEE, JUST 14 BRITISH OVERSEAS TERRITORIES REMAINED, A TINY REMNANT OF THE EMPIRE.

Bermuda, with barely 65,000 inhabitants, is the most populous Overseas Territory. The smallest is The Pitcairn Islands, in the Pacific, which has 56 residents according to its last census.

In place of the Empire is the Commonwealth, and the Queen is its head, a role that means as much to her as the British crown. She delivers her Commonwealth Day address in March each year, and since 1997 has attended every biennial meeting of the Commonwealth Heads of Government in countries around the world. She has officially opened every Commonwealth Games since her reign began, with two exceptions: 1966 in Kingston, Jamaica, which was too close to the World Cup in England, and 2010 in Delhi, where she was represented by the Prince of Wales.

Of the Commonwealth's 54 member states, all but two were once part of the British Empire. Fifteen, apart from the United Kingdom itself, are realms and still recognize the Queen as their monarch and head of state. They range in size from Australia and Canada down to the tiny Polynesian island of Tuvalu.

Even before she took the throne, the Queen knew the importance of the Commonwealth. In 1947, as Princess Elizabeth, she made a twenty-first birthday address during a tour of South Africa and dedicated her life to the service of the Commonwealth. "If we all go forward together with an unwavering faith," she said, "a high courage and a quiet heart, we shall be able to make of this ancient Commonwealth, which we love so dearly, an even grander thing – more free, more prosperous, more happy and a more powerful influence for good in the world – than it has been in the greatest days of our forefathers."

Shortly after the coronation, in November 1953, the Queen and Prince Philip set off on a tour of the Commonwealth that would now be inconceivable. It lasted five and a half long months, far exceeding their previous tour of Canada and even the planned state visit to Australia and New Zealand that had to be abandoned when the King died. The Queen took her coronation dress to wear for state openings of Parliament in Australia, New Zealand and Ceylon.

ABOVE Standards of Commonwealth nations which were carried in the Queen's coronation procession, representing Australia (top) and Canada (bottom).

The itinerary for this tour took the royal couple first to Bermuda and Jamaica and then on through the Panama Canal to Fiji, Tonga, the Coco Islands (administered by Burma), Aden, Uganda, Malta, Gibraltar, Australia, New Zealand and finally Ceylon, now Sri Lanka. It was a journey that exposed the new Queen to an extraordinary range of cultures. Today, she flies when she goes abroad. In 1953, her progress was rather statelier, aboard the royal yacht HMS *Gothic*.

The key part of the tour began in New Zealand, a country where enthusiasm for the coronation had reached fever pitch as people watched, not on live television but on newsreel films flown out for distribution to local cinemas. Elizabeth and Philip, like the Duke and Duchess of Cambridge nearly 60 years later, were portrayed as the new, modern face of the monarchy, a departure from the old, more distant royal family. New Zealanders at the time fretted about their links with Britain and their ties with the rest of the Commonwealth. Their new Queen restored their confidence.

ABOVE The Queen's coronation in June 1953. Some 8,000 dignitaries filled Westminster Abbey to see the 25-year-old British ruler crowned.

RIGHT The Queen and the Duke of Edinburgh in Hamilton, Bermuda, the first stop on their epic tour of the Commonwealth, in 1953.

BELOW Scout's honour: the Queen is sheltered from the sun as she is greeted by a Canadian boy scout, 1959.

RIGHT A map of the first part of the Commonwealth Tour which the Queen and the Duke of Edinburgh undertook very soon after the Coronation in 1953. Together they visited almost every Commonwealth state, with the Queen wearing her Coronation dress on several occasions as she opened new sessions of various parliaments in countries such as Australia and New Zealand.

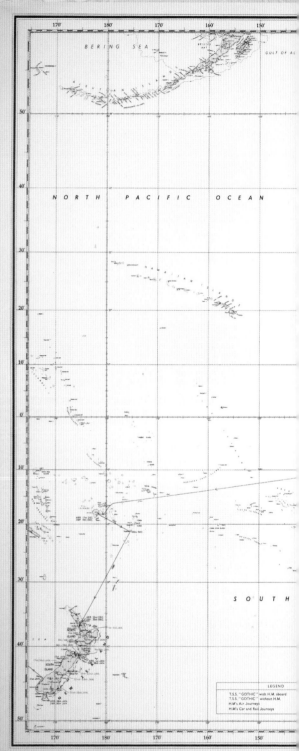

ROYAL TOUR
1953-54
OUTWARD JOURNEY

On 3 February 1954, the Queen and Prince Philip stepped ashore at Sydney, Australia. The Queen has now been to Australia 16 times and made her most recent tour in 2011, in the run-up to her Diamond Jubilee year. But there has never been anything to match that epic first journey. It lasted two months, during which the royal couple took more than 30 domestic flights spanning 10,000 miles. They made more than 200 journeys by car, 130 hours in all, and travelled 2,000 miles on Australia's roads. Royal trains were laid on as well. Every state capital but one was visited, along with 70 country towns. It is estimated that three-quarters of the Australian population turned out to see them, and at one memorable event at Melbourne Cricket Ground they appeared before 70,000 ex-servicemen and women.

ABOVE The Queen with Commonwealth leaders at Buckingham Palace in 1961. South Africa's Hendrik Verwoed (second from left) withdrew from the Commonwealth after dissension over apartheid.

LEFT A necklace and bracelet given to the Queen on her visit to Ghana and put on display at Buckingham Palace.

RIGHT The Queen with President Kwame Nkrumah during the royal tour of Ghana, 1961.

In that southern-hemisphere summer of '54, Australia was gripped by a royal frenzy. When her father went there in 1927, the talk had been about his daughter, the Princess the Australians nicknamed "Betty". Now, they finally had a chance to see her in person and few could resist. The Prime Minister of the day, Robert Menzies, wrote of "the profound and passionate feelings of loyalty and devotion".

Moods change, of course, and 45 years later Australians went to the polls to vote on getting rid of the monarchy and turning their nation into a republic. Nearly 55 per cent of those polled said "no" to a republic, an affirmation of loyalty to the crown but hardly the level of support the Queen enjoyed on that heady first visit. The year after the referendum, she returned to Australia, this time on her thirteenth visit. In a speech at Sydney Opera House she made it clear she viewed the future of the monarchy in Australia as a matter "for you, the Australia people, and you alone to decide". She added, "I shall continue faithfully to serve to the best of my ability as Queen of Australia."

The Queen remains Head of the Commonwealth, but it is not a position she holds by right. And the Commonwealth, of course, is no longer "British". It changed to the "Commonwealth of Nations" in 1949, after Indian independence began a prolonged debate about exactly what should happen as the old British Empire began to disintegrate. The process has not always been easy and the role of the monarch not always clear. But many in the Commonwealth believe that it is the Queen's non-political, symbolic presence that has held the organization together.

Britain's colonies started to break away from their old imperial master with increasing pace during the first decade of the Queen's reign. Some chose to retain her as head of state, others did not. A few, like Swaziland and Tonga, have their own monarchs as head of state. There was political diversity, too. Not all member nations maintained a commitment to the Commonwealth ideals of freedom and democracy.

BELOW The Queen entertained President Eisenhower at Balmoral in Scotland in August 1959 where she served him drop scones to which he took a liking. In January of the following year, the Queen sent her recipe for the scones to the President in a letter.

OPPOSITE Royal procession: the Queen carried in style on an elephant during the tour of India, 1961.

MENU

Date...

DROP SCONES

Ingredients

4 teacups flour

4 tablespoons caster sugar

2 teacups milk

2 whole eggs

2 teaspoons bi-carbonate soda

3 teaspoons cream of tartar

2 tablespoons melted butter

Beat eggs, sugar and about half the milk together, add flour, and mix well together adding remainder of milk as required, also bi-carbonate and cream of tartar, fold in the melted butter.

Enough for 16 people

The Commonwealth

The Queen's first major Commonwealth dilemma occurred towards the end of 1961. Earlier that year she had toured India, first among nations of the old British Empire to declare independence and then to become a republic. To underline the break from Britain, Elizabeth was invited as Queen of the United Kingdom, not as Head of the Commonwealth. There was concern about the reception she would get, not least because of the violence that had marred the partition of India and Pakistan. In the end the only controversy centred round Prince Philip's part in a tiger hunt. Half a million people turned out on the streets of Delhi to see the royal couple.

But now, in November 1961, the Queen was bound for Ghana, a visit postponed from the previous year because of the birth of her third child, Andrew. The situation in Ghana had changed uncomfortably in the intervening months. Kwame Nkrumah, who led his country to independence, had moved towards the dictatorship of a one-party state. It presented the British government with a dilemma: should the Queen visit a country with what was perceived as an unacceptable regime? And would she be safe to do so? There was another question, too: if the Queen cancelled, would Nkrumah take Ghana out of the Commonwealth and precipitate its collapse?

The Queen certainly did not want the trip called off, and reports at the time suggested she argued forcefully that it would be difficult to continue as Head of the Commonwealth if she were not allowed to go. The Queen, after

all, must remain above politics. The trip went ahead, with the Queen taking the opportunity to address Ghanaians about the importance of the Commonwealth "family". Their state-controlled press responded by bestowing on her an unlikely title: "the greatest socialist monarch in the world".

Many years later, events in Africa again embroiled the Queen in controversy over the role of the Commonwealth. This time the issue was the white-controlled Rhodesia of Ian Smith. It was 1979 and Britain's Prime Minister Margaret Thatcher was reluctant to attend the Commonwealth Heads of Government Meeting in Zambia because of widespread African opposition to her policy on Rhodesia. In the end, she did go to the conference, but not its opening ceremony, although it was the Queen who was given much of the credit for what was achieved

there. Her relationship with influential African leaders like Kenneth Kaunda, Hastings Banda and Julius Nyerere was seen as crucial in persuading them to take part in talks that subsequently brought an end to the Rhodesia crisis and the creation of the new state of Zimbabwe.

Sir Shridath "Sonny" Ramphal, the Commonwealth Secretary-General at the time, said the Queen had an understanding of post-colonial Commonwealth leaders that the Foreign Office did not. He wrote: "She grew up with them, understood them and related to them. They could talk with her and she wasn't talking down. She got to know them very well. Even at the times when the British government was at odds with many of these leaders, she was able to understand their point of view without taking sides, and managed to convey to them that she did."

OPPOSITE ABOVE Queen Elizabeth recording her Commonwealth Day message at Buckingham Palace, 2000.

OPPOSITE BELOW "G'day ma'am": the Queen with members of the Australian hockey team at the Commonwealth Games, Manchester, 2002.

ABOVE LEFT African walkabout: the Queen and Prince Andrew in Dar Es Salaam, Tanzania, July 1979.

ABOVE RIGHT Nelson Mandela welcomes the Queen to South Africa in 1995; it was her first visit there for 48 years.

Royal Duties

THE SIXTIES WERE THE DECADE WHEN BOB DYLAN SANG OF TIMES A-CHANGIN' AND A PRIME MINISTER PROMISED A REVOLUTION FORGED IN THE WHITE HEAT OF TECHNOLOGY. THERE WAS A NEW MOOD IN BRITAIN AND THE TRADITIONAL SYMBOLS OF AUTHORITY WERE INCREASINGLY CHALLENGED. THE DEATH PENALTY WAS ABOLISHED, CENSORSHIP IN THEATRES WAS BROUGHT TO AN END AND THE VOTING AGE WAS REDUCED FROM 21 TO 18. IN SOCIAL ATTITUDES, AS MUCH AS IN MUSIC, IT WAS THE SWINGING SIXTIES.

The royal family recognized those changing times, too. The Queen had lost little of her popularity – around half the population tuned in to her 1960 Christmas broadcast – but the age of deference, of unquestioning loyalty, was over. As the decade came to an end, she was to allow the public a window into her life that would until then have been completely unimaginable.

It was also the decade when the royal family became complete, when the "us four" of her father King George VI found an echo in "we six". Prince Andrew was born in February 1960, and was followed four years later by the Queen's fourth child, Edward, who was born in the Belgian Suite at Buckingham Palace, where many years later her grandson the Duke of Cambridge was to spend his wedding night. The Archbishop of Canterbury, Dr Michael Ramsey, spoke of "a Christian family united, happy and setting to all an example of what the words home and family most truly meant". There was a 15-year

gap between the Queen's eldest and youngest children. When Edward was born, Prince Charles was enduring what he has admitted was hardly the happiest time of his life, at Gordonstoun School in Scotland. Eton had seemed the natural choice, but Prince Philip was keen to avoid the elitist tag it would have bestowed.

British prime ministers, however, did by tradition go to Eton or, in the case of Winston Churchill, to its equally elitist rival Harrow. These were the men Queen Elizabeth had dealt with in the weekly audiences at Buckingham Palace: Churchill, the elder statesman and guiding light in her early years on the throne, Sir Anthony Eden, Sir Harold Macmillan and Sir Alec Douglas Home, formerly the Earl of Home; all Conservatives, all linked to the aristocracy and all pillars of the British establishment. But in the general election of October 1964, 13 years of Tory rule were brought to an end and for the first time the Queen had a Labour prime minister, Harold Wilson.

ABOVE The Queen and the Duke of Edinburgh with Prince Andrew and an infant Prince Edward after Trooping the Colour in 1964.

OPPOSITE Best of friends: the Queen with Labour Prime Minister Harold Wilson in 1969. Despite the difference in their backgrounds, they enjoyed a warm relationship.

Wilson, author of that "white heat of technology" speech, was very different to his predecessors. There was no blue blood in his veins: his father was a chemist, his mother a schoolteacher, and he was himself a grammar-school boy. Inevitably, there was much speculation about how the Queen and the new Prime Minister would get on. The answer was famously. As the weekly prime ministerial audiences stretched to two hours and beyond, Wilson found himself impressed by the Queen's grasp of issues of state and she apparently relished her discussions with a man so determined to bring change to the country.

If Harold Wilson himself was a professed royalist, others in his cabinet were less enthusiastic about the monarchy. Richard Crossman had made no secret of his disdain for both the institution and the individual, railing at traditions like the "kissing of hands" for new ministers and the demand that meetings of the Queen's Privy Council were held at a place and time of her convenience. But, as one senior palace official has told me, even ardent republicans often find themselves in awe in the presence of the Queen, and Richard Crossman was no exception. His

OPPOSITE The royal procession at the State Opening of Parliament in 1970. Prince Charles and Princess Anne are behind their parents.

ABOVE The Queen at the Ideal Home Exhibition in 1965, the golden jubilee year of the National Federation of Women's Institutes.

diaries make reference to their "cosy chats", and he added glowingly, "She laughs with her whole face."

Tony Benn was not so readily won over, but he too seemed charmed by the Queen when, as Postmaster General, he presented her with a proposition to remove her image from postage stamps. "I went back to the House of Commons feeling absolutely on top of the world," he wrote after a disarmingly receptive audience with the Queen. In the end, the Queen's image stayed in place and Tony Benn was forced to concede, "It's probably rather foolish of me to go knocking my head against a brick wall."

If the Queen was able to charm even left-wing ministers, attitudes towards the monarchy were shifting. Cinemas stopped playing the national anthem, the audience for the Christmas broadcast began to fall and the abolition of rules preventing the portrayal of the monarch on stage heralded the spread of satire in which members of the royal family were openly lampooned.

BELOW US President John F Kennedy and his glamorous wife, Jackie, are welcomed to Buckingham Palace on their state visit in 1961.

Throughout it all, Elizabeth upheld the traditions and responsibilities of the royal life into which she had now settled, duties that were a mixture of the routine and the ceremonial. The most colourful event, and also the most constitutionally significant, is the State Opening of Parliament. The Queen travels from Buckingham Palace in a state coach and the ceremony is held in the House of Lords. No monarch has set foot in the House of Commons since 1642, when Charles I tried to arrest five MPs. There remain symbolic reminders of past tensions between crown and Parliament. The Yeomen of the Guard search the cellars at the Houses of Parliament, as they have since the days

ABOVE Hard at work: the Queen at her desk, opening an official government box containing documents sent for her attention, 1959.

RIGHT Elizabeth visits the Welsh mining village of Aberfan, where 116 children and 28 adults had been killed in an accident, in October 1966.

LEFT We did it:
the Queen presents
the World Cup to
England captain
Bobby Moore, 1966.

of the Guy Fawkes gunpowder plot of 1605. A government whip is still held as a "hostage" at Buckingham Palace to guarantee the monarch's safe return.

The Queen's other public engagements include Trooping the Colour, held in June to celebrate her birthday, the Royal Ascot race meeting and the Remembrance Day ceremony in November. Occasionally, as in the 1960s, there are special additions to the her schedule. In 1966, she presented the World Cup to England captain Bobby Moore at Wembley stadium, and three years later the Investiture of the Prince of Wales was held at Caernarfon Castle.

In 1968, the Queen made a new appointment to her Buckingham Palace staff, and the way she was portrayed to the public began to change. For 20 years media relations at the palace had been in the hands of a retired naval officer, Commander Richard Colville. He gave little ground in requests for access to the royal family and was known on Fleet Street as "the abominable no-man". On his retirement, Colville was replaced by William Heseltine, an Australian who had worked as a political adviser in his homeland before joining the palace press office.

Heseltine recognized the need for the royal family to appear more accessible and for some of the traditional barriers to be broken. Commander Colville had regarded television with horror and the Queen had all too often appeared uncomfortable in front of the cameras. The BBC even considered scrapping her televised Christmas address and reverting to radio. However, Heseltine had a very different view. He believed television was crucial to the Queen's continuing popularity and must be accepted as a part of royal life.

The consequence was extraordinary and transfixed the nation. Suddenly, cameras were invited behind the doors that had been so firmly closed to them. The result was *Royal Family*, a 90-minute documentary that was shown in June 1969, first on the BBC and then ITV. It was edited from 43 hours of film shot over the course of a year and followed some of the royal family's most private moments.

By the standards of today's fly-on-the-wall documentaries, *Royal Family* was hardly a controversial exposé, but at the time it caused

LEFT The Queen with members of her Privy Council, a scene from the 1969 BBC documentary *Royal Family*.

BELOW The Prince of Wales is crowned by his mother at his investiture at Caernarfon Castle in Wales, 1969.

OVERLEAF The royal family trying to look natural at Windsor in 1969. From left: Prince Edward, Prince Philip, the Queen, Princess Anne, Prince Charles and Prince Andrew.

a sensation. Here were the Queen and Prince Philip giggling with their children over dinner, or sharing a family barbecue in the grounds of Balmoral, with the Duke of Edinburgh cooking the sausages. The royal biographer Ben Pimlott observed: "People are said to dream about the Queen coming to tea. It was as though she had. Yet if the film smashed icons, it did not destroy the stereotypes." Perhaps not, but for all the jacket-and-tie formality of its royal gatherings and the often stilted conversations, the film allowed the Queen's subjects at last to see behind the façade of royalty and to glimpse its routine, everyday life – and also to see the Queen as a normal, loving mother. In one of the most affecting scenes she takes a young Prince Edward to the village shop in Balmoral to buy an ice cream, warning him to be careful about making "a gooey mess" as they get back in the car.

Should *Royal Family* have been allowed? The Queen was said to have been happy with it and Prince Philip had always been enthusiastic.

"I think it is quite wrong that there should be a sense of remoteness of majesty," he said in an interview with *The Times*. " If people see whoever it happens to be, whatever head of state, as individuals, as people, I think it makes it much easier for them to accept the system or feel part of the system."

Nevertheless, there were misgivings. Princess Anne talked about it in a television interview years later, commenting, "I always thought it was a rotten idea. The attention that had been brought on one ever since one was a child, you just don't want any more. The last thing you needed was greater access."

As the Sixties came to an end, the Queen appeared accessible as never before. But she had, as Ben Pimlott put it, "let the genie out of the bottle". The media had been allowed the insight they craved and they wanted more. The royal family was entering a new and not altogether comfortable age of public scrutiny.

The Queen's Year

A NEW WORD ENTERED THE ROYAL LEXICON IN 1970: "WALKABOUT". IT WAS COINED BY A *DAILY MAIL* REPORTER COVERING THE TOUR TO AUSTRALIA AND NEW ZEALAND WITH WHICH THE QUEEN AND PRINCE PHILIP STARTED THE DECADE AND IT HAPPENED IN NEW ZEALAND'S CAPITAL CITY, WELLINGTON.

Walkabouts are a routine feature of almost every royal visit now, but back in 1970 the walkabout was a novelty, something the royal family just did not do. They would meet and talk to invited guests, certainly, but strolling along the street and stopping to chat with members of the general public was not part of the programme. The royal family's popularity had unquestionably been boosted by the documentary about them shown the year before, and William Heseltine, the Queen's press secretary who had been so keen on that, was again the prime mover. He persuaded the Queen and Prince Philip to leave their car on their way to an official event in Wellington and mingle with people who had lined the streets to see them.

The Queen now met more and more members of the general public at home, too. She had increased the number of garden parties at Buckingham Palace to three a year, with up to 8,000 guests attending each one, and there was another garden party at Holyroodhouse in Edinburgh.

The Seventies were also the decade of the street party, a time when people in their hundreds of thousands hung out the bunting, put up trestle tables, closed their roads and organized the sort of gatherings unseen since

BELOW Hori Paki, who was 104 years old, greeting the Queen on her tour of New Zealand, 1970.

OPPOSITE The marriage of Princess Anne and Captain Mark Phillips, November 1973. The bride was attended by Lady Sarah Armstrong-Jones and Prince Edward.

the coronation. The cause of the celebrations was the Queen's Silver Jubilee in 1977, a year when Britain needed a good party to lift the gloom caused by industrial unrest and economic uncertainty.

Jubilee celebrations began in earnest in June and lasted throughout the summer. The Queen launched them by lighting a bonfire atop a hill near Windsor Castle, the signal for 100 other fires to be lit across the country. The following day, she travelled in a carriage procession to St Paul's Cathedral for a special jubilee service. Prince Philip was at her side in the state coach and the Prince of Wales followed on horseback in the uniform of colonel of the Welsh Guards. Following the service at St Paul's, the Queen went on what will perhaps be remembered as her most tumultuous walkabout, through the streets of the City of London, an event still remembered with the Jubilee Walkway route through London which is signposted with silver-coloured metal discs bearing a crown and set in the ground along the way. She toured other British cities as well and, despite fears over security, went to Northern Ireland.

The street parties went on through it all. In London alone, there were more than 4,000 of them, with neighbours uniting as they had not done since the days of the war. As a BBC reporter at the time I remember covering parties in the Yorkshire mining towns of Castleford and Pontefract. They seem now to be reminders of a lost age, of a spirit of community that largely disappeared as coal mines were closed in the years that followed. Not everyone who went to those parties was a devoted monarchist, of course, but the Queen's 25 years on the throne gave them a reason to celebrate that they readily accepted.

The Queen had another reason to celebrate in that jubilee year, with the arrival of her first grandchild. Peter Phillips was born on 15 November, the day after the fourth wedding anniversary of his parents, Princess Anne and Captain Mark Phillips. They had married, in 1973, at Westminster Abbey, a couple with a

LEFT The Queen chatting to guests on the lawn at Buckingham Palace during a garden party in 1979.

BELOW The Queen and Prince Philip, who were accompanied by Prince Charles, arrive at the Paris home of the Duke and Duchess of Windsor in 1972.

shared love of horses and a shared expertise as equestrians. The Princess had a string of sporting titles to her name. She had been voted BBC Sports Personality of the Year in 1971 and went on to compete in the 1976 Montreal Olympics. Captain Phillips had an even more illustrious career, winning a gold medal at the 1972 Olympics in Munich and winning the Badminton Horse Trials on four occasions.

If the royal family had occasions to celebrate in the 1970s, there were also more sombre and difficult occasions. The first occurred early in the decade, in 1972, when the Queen and Prince Philip paid a five-day visit to France. It was decided that now, 36 years after his abdication as King Edward VIII, the Queen could finally visit her uncle David, the Duke of Windsor, at the Paris home he shared with his wife, the former Wallis Simpson. The Duchess of Windsor greeted the royal visitors, the Queen, Prince Philip and the Prince of Wales, and led them to meet the former King, now confined to a wheelchair and painfully thin. It was reported that when the Queen asked him how he was the Duke, who had risen to his feet, replied, "Not so bad." But he died ten days later.

The body of the former King was flown back to England, and for two days before the funeral service the coffin was displayed at St George's Chapel, Windsor Castle and viewed by 60,000 people who filed past. The Duchess of Windsor joined members of the royal family at the service and was accommodated at Buckingham Palace, although Queen Elizabeth the Queen Mother did not attend a dinner for her. The Duchess herself died 14 years later and was buried beside her husband at Frogmore, near Windsor Castle.

The royal family was also made sharply aware of the threats they faced. In 1974, four people, including two police officers, were shot and wounded during an attempt to kidnap Princess Anne as she was driven along the Mall with her husband, Captain Mark Phillips. The gunman asked her to go with him and the Princess famously responded, "Not bloody likely!"

As the Seventies drew to a close, the Queen and her family suffered an even more bitter blow. In August 1979, Lord Louis Mountbatten was murdered by the IRA when his boat was blown up off the coast of County Sligo near his family home of Classiebawn Castle in the Republic of Ireland. Two of his relatives and a 15-year-old boy were also killed. Lord Mountbatten had close ties with the royal family. He was a great-grandson of Queen Victoria and a cousin of the Queen. He was also Prince Philip's uncle and particularly close to the Prince of Wales, who wrote afterwards that "life will never be the same now he has gone". Lord Mountbatten's views may not

always have been shared by the royal family, but he had been a significant and often influential presence in their lives. His death was a source of intense personal grief.

There were political as well as personal upheavals for the Queen to confront as well, with four separate prime ministers attending audiences with her at Buckingham Palace during the 1970s. Harold Wilson was replaced by Edward Heath after an unexpected Conservative victory in June 1970. Dealings between the Queen and Heath were less relaxed. The new Tory Prime Minister was more business-like, less at ease with small talk.

ABOVE Star quality: the Queen and Barbara Streisand at the London premiere of the film *Funny Lady*, 1975.

Four years later, the Queen was opening the Australian Parliament in Canberra as Britain went to the polls in a snap election called by Edward Heath at the height of an industrial crisis that caused coal shortages, power cuts and the notorious three-day week. The Queen returned to Buckingham Palace, jet-lagged and exhausted, two days after the polls closed. Labour had won most seats although not an overall majority, but it was four days before Edward Heath was forced to admit failure in his attempts to form a coalition government with the Liberals and step down.

Harold Wilson's second term as Prime Minister, and those warm weekly chats with the Queen, came to an end when he announced his retirement in March 1976. It was a mark of her fondness for him that she attended a farewell dinner at Number 10 Downing Street, an honour she has only bestowed on one other departing prime minister, Winston Churchill. Wilson was replaced by James Callaghan, another Labour leader whose devotion to the monarchy was at odds with many in his party. So began another comfortable working relationship: in Callaghan's own words, their conversations "could roam anywhere over a wide range of social as well as political and international topics".

The Seventies had been a relatively calm era for the monarchy. There was little serious controversy, a generally even level of public support and, apart from the divorce of Princess Margaret and Lord Snowdon in 1976, little to generate uncomfortable levels of interest from media. But times of great change lay ahead, for both Queen and country. On 4 May 1979, Margaret Thatcher arrived at Buckingham Palace for the formal kissing of hands with the Queen to become the country's first woman Prime Minister. As a new decade began, she was to bring transformation and upheaval to Britain, just as a new member of the royal family would to the House of Windsor.

OPPOSITE Four generations of the royal family at Buckingham Palace after the christening of Princess Anne's son, Peter Phillips, 1977.

RIGHT The original sketch by Hardy Amies for the outfit that the Queen wore on the day of her Silver Jubilee celebrations, which can be seen in the photo below.

LEFT Silver Jubilee: the Queen waves to crowds from the balcony of Buckingham Palace, June 1977.

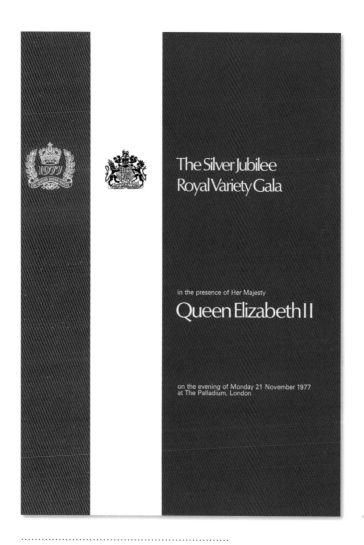

The Silver Jubilee
Royal Variety Gala

in the presence of Her Majesty

Queen Elizabeth II

on the evening of Monday 21 November 1977
at The Palladium, London

The Silver Jubilee Royal Variety Gala

Bob Hope
as Host

Julie Andrews

Paul Anka

Pam Ayres

Harry Belafonte

Brotherhood of Man

Tommy Cooper

Alan King

Cleo Laine with John Dankworth and John Williams

Little and Large

Shirley MacLaine

Jim Henson's Muppets
Choreography by Gillian Lynne

Rudolph Nureyev with Yokio Morishipa
and other Guest Stars

Jack Parnell and his Orchestra

Bob Hope appears by courtesy of Texaco
Total production conceived and devised by Garry Smith & Dwight Hemion

ABOVE, OPPOSITE AND OVERLEAF An extract of pages from the 1977 programme for the Silver Jubilee Royal Variety Performance which was held on 21 November at the Palladium Theatre in London. The Royal Variety Performance has been cancelled only once – in 1956 – when owing to the mounting crisis over the Suez Canal, it was called off. The Royal Variety Performance celebrated its 100th anniversary in 2012.

BOB HOPE

Bob Hope was born in Eltham, England, and went to the United States at the age of four. He entered show business in 1924, hoping to make a fortune with a song-and-dance act. The combination of natural wit, hard work, wise choice of material and—by his own admission—good luck, made his dream come true.

A successful vaudeville career was followed by an equally bright career in Broadway musical comedy; on Radio as the star of his own comedy series; in motion pictures, and, since 1950, on NBC-TV.

Married to the former Dolores Reade, he is the father of four adopted children, Tony, Linda, Nora and Kelley, and the grandfather of four, Zachary and Miranda Hope, Andrew Lane and Alicia Hope McCullagh.

Known in the United States of America as one of the country's best known philanthropists. As a boy he was an indifferent scholar; today he holds honorary degrees from thirty-nine seats of education and more than 2,000 citations for his humanitarian and professional efforts, including the Medal of Freedom, the Congressional Gold Medal, four special Oscar citations, the Criss Award, to name but a few. Bob Hope, star of "The Bob Hope Specials" for NBC-TV network was named last February for the third consecutive year the "People's Choice Award as Male Entertainer of the Year". He is now in his fifty-third year in show business.

A legend in his own time, Bob Hope had become a much loved figure in the world itself and the world of entertainment.

JULIE ANDREWS

In defining the magic of the multi talented Julie Andrews, an astute journalist made this comment, ". . . the lady is not just a great star, she is a whirling, dazzling constellation. Julie is not just an ordinary movie personality, she is a phenomenon".

Back in 1954, when a complete unknown to American audiences, Miss Andrews starred in her first Broadway production "The Boy Friend". Subsequently, she became the toast of Broadway in the title role of Eliza Doolittle in Lerner and Loewe's "My Fair Lady", which set a record for the longest run on Broadway.

After 18 months in London with "My Fair Lady", and a brief hiatus to guest on a few television shows, Julie returned to Broadway as the star of "Camelot".

In her motion picture debut, she won the Academy Award as Best Actress of 1964 in the title role of "Mary Poppins" for Walt Disney.

She was again nominated in 1965 by the Academy for Best Actress for her portrayal of Maria Trapp in "The Sound of Music", which set a record as the industry's all time top grosser.

Julie Andrews' career is based upon years of study and hard work. It began at the age of twelve, when she astounded a London Hippodrome audience with an operatic aria in the "Starlight Roof" revue. It was while appearing in the pantomime "Cinderella" at the London Palladium that Julie's big break came.

Vida Hope, who had produced and directed the London production of the hit musical "The Boy Friend" was searching for an actress to play the lead role on Broadway; Julie was approached, and reluctantly accepted, since she had never been out of England or away from her family and friends before. She was asked to sign a two year contract, but insisted on a one year contract.

Towards the end of a very successful year in "The Boy Friend", Julie received a call from a representative of the composing and producing team of Alan Jay Lerner and Frederick Loewe. They were preparing "My Fair Lady", a musical version of George Bernard Shaw's "Pygmalion" and were interested in Julie for the role of Eliza Doolittle.

She auditioned for the role and was signed immediately. The play opened out of town to rave notices and when it came to Broadway, the acclaim was overwhelming. The rest is theatrical history, for the musical enjoyed one of Broadway's longest runs. Julie returned to England to play in the London run of the show.

TOMMY COOPER

RIGHT The Queen
greets well-wishers
during a Silver
Jubilee walkabout
in Camberwell,
south London.

Born in Caerphilly, South Wales. Moved to Exeter when only a few weeks o
then moved to Southampton until joining the Army. Was in the Horse Guard>
   Entered the profession in 1947, a few months after leaving the Army.
cabaret and several TV shows. First TV date was December 24th, 1947 in the
Party. Next two years spent touring the smaller Variety Theatres, the first st
Hall, Islington, November 1948. During those two years he did a CSE tou
Windmill and a Pantomime, where he played Ugly Sister. Appeared at the Lo
Des Folies" for the entire run from March 1951 until February 1952. Starred
Magic" every fortnight from March to June 1952. Had a wonderful Pr
Funniest Man in Britain". London Palladium debut in July 1952 when he stole
then his first tour for Moss Empires as one of the tops of the bill. March 19
where he proved himself a superb all round comic.
   Booked once again for the London Palladium for Coronation Season 195
in 1954, when he appeared at the fabulous Hotel Flamingo, Las Vegas. Am
"the highspot of the show". And so, for the past thirty years, Tommy has grac
it can fairly be said that this most lovable and popular comedian, with his
humour, with his comedy magic has done everything there is to be done in she
endeared himself to all.

JIM HENSON'S MUPPETS

Jim Henson's Muppets, that delightful company of amiable monsters and fantastic fauna, have such distinct
personalities of their own that it's hard to believe they need human help to perform. But they do. They
couldn't function without the people behind them—or more accurately (most Muppets are manipulated from
underneath on the arms of the performer) below them.
   The Muppets are in—and on—good hands, the best. Jim Henson, Frank Oz, Jerry Nelson, Richard
Hunt and Dave Goelz are performers of such versatility and skill that their Muppet charges have come the
most widely known and highest rated puppet group in the world.
   In its first year on television, "The Muppet Show" has won award after award, including the Golden
Rose of Montreux, bestowed on the light entertainment TV programme judged the international best. Seen
throughout the United States and in over 100 other markets, the show has caused pandemic excitement
known as "Muppetmania".
   The Muppets of television are constantly on public view; everyone knows them. But the artistes who
move them, speak for them, imbue them with their vitality and charm, are never seen on camera.

Public Perceptions

LADY DIANA SPENCER WAS 19 YEARS OLD WHEN HER
ENGAGEMENT TO THE PRINCE OF WALES WAS ANNOUNCED.
WHEN HE MARRIED THE COUPLE FIVE MONTHS LATER, THE
ARCHBISHOP OF CANTERBURY SAID, "HERE IS THE STUFF OF
WHICH FAIRY TALES ARE MADE." THE QUEEN AND PRINCE
PHILIP WERE DELIGHTED, YET THE SHY, DEMURE YOUNG
WOMAN THEY SO EAGERLY WELCOMED BROUGHT TO THE
MODERN ROYAL FAMILY AN UPHEAVAL MATCHED ONLY BY
THE ABDICATION CRISIS OF THE 1930S.

ABOVE Moment of crisis: the Queen calms
her horse Burmese after shots were fired at the
Trooping the Colour, 1981.

But while the abdication crisis had lasted
a few short months, the House of
Windsor now embarked on nearly two
decades of controversy, scandal and intrusion on
a scale unimaginable in the serene early years of
Elizabeth's reign.

The omens of a difficult decade appeared
early in the 1980s. The first came in June
1981, as the Queen rode down the Mall on
her way to the annual Trooping the Colour
ceremony in Horse Guards Parade, which
marks the monarch's official birthday and is
one of the ceremonial highlights of the royal
year. Among the crowds lining the mall was
17-year-old Marcus Serjeant. He suddenly
stepped forward brandishing a revolver at the
Queen and fired six shots that fortunately
turned out to be blank rounds. The Queen
was riding her charger Burmese, which reared
alarmingly before Elizabeth brought her

under control. The Queen was
praised for her composure and
Serjeant later told the police, " I
wanted to be famous. I wanted
to be somebody."

It was not the only breach of
royal security. The following year,
asleep in her bed at Buckingham
Palace, the Queen was woken up
by the footsteps of an intruder.
It transpired that Michael Fagan
had broken into the Palace before
and stolen a bottle of wine.
This time, he was able to walk
unchallenged into the Queen's
private apartment, where he wanted to talk about
his family problems. The Queen was calm at the
time, but later furious about the lapse in security.

There was a third, far more serious incident
less than two weeks later when the IRA

detonated a nail bomb in Hyde Park as the Household Cavalry rode by on their way to the Changing of the Guard at Buckingham Palace. Four soldiers were killed and seven of their horses. Within two hours there was another bomb, beneath a bandstand in Regent's Park where bandsmen of the Royal Green Jackets were playing tunes from the musical *Oliver*. Seven of them were killed.

But on the morning of 29 July 1981, there was not cloud in the sky as people prepared to celebrate what the newspapers had inevitably dubbed "the wedding of the century". As on so many previous royal occasions, Britain was sorely in need of something to lighten the gloom. The spring and summer had been marred by violent riots on the streets of London and Liverpool. London was packed for the wedding, with upwards of three-quarters of a million people lining the route from Buckingham Palace to St Paul's Cathedral. Many had slept out overnight to be sure of a good view of the wedding procession, and they were not disappointed. Nearly one billion people around the world watched on television.

It is easy now, through the prism of subsequent events, to see the wedding of Charles and Diana in a different light. However, on the day no one challenged the Archbishop's use of the words "fairy tale". Diana arrived at St Paul's in the Queen's glass coach and emerged to a roar from the crowd as they saw the wedding dress with its 25-foot-long train. Here was the perfect royal bride. The Prince of Wales had been linked to several attractive young women, but it appeared that in Lady Diana Spencer the nation had at last found its ideal future Queen.

BELOW Safely home: Prince Andrew returns to Portsmouth after the Falklands War, 1982.

OVERLEAF The official family photograph at the wedding of the Prince and Princess of Wales, July 1981.

EⅡR

The Lord Chamberlain is
commanded by Her Majesty to invite

....

....

to a Garden Party at Buckingham Palace
on Wednesday, 14th July, 1982 from 4 to 6 p.m.

Morning Dress, Uniform or Lounge Suit

LEFT An invitation to one of the garden parties held at Buckingham Palace in 1982. Garden parties have been held at the Palace since the 1860s. They were originally known as "Breakfasts" even though they took place in the afternoon. In the 1950s, the number held each year was increased from two to three. There is also one held at the Palace of Holyroodhouse during the weeks that the Queen spends in Scotland.

BELOW Margaret Thatcher and husband Denis leave the Grand Hotel, Brighton, after an IRA bomb attack, 1984.

The media's already healthy appetite for stories about Diana became insatiable, the more so as the marriage clearly began to founder. Any vestige of restraint in covering the royal family finally disappeared. If a modest television documentary more than a decade before had briefly drawn back the curtains, the doors and windows were now flung wide open. The Queen and her family were fair game.

The stories were political as well as personal, frequently revolving around what was perceived to be a strained relationship between the Queen and Margaret Thatcher. In her 1983 Christmas broadcast, the Queen, as she has done so often, spoke up for the Commonwealth. It was hardly Mrs Thatcher's favourite organization, and there was tension over Britain's reluctance to agree to Commonwealth demands for sanctions against the apartheid regime in South Africa. The Queen's view that one of the Commonwealth's main aims was "to make an effective contribution towards redressing the economic balance between nations" did not sit well with Downing Street's view of the world. But what reportedly irritated the Prime Minister most was the Queen's assertion that the gap between

the world's richest and poorest would not be closed "until we hear less about nationalism and more about interdependence".

Three years later *The Sunday Times* reported that the Queen found Mrs Thatcher's policies to be "uncaring, confrontational and socially divisive". She was said to have been uneasy about the handling of the 1984 miners' strike as well as continuing disagreements with the Commonwealth. Buckingham Palace knew the story was to be published but did not attempt to stop it, arguing there would have been no point. The days when newspaper editors could be warned off or even swayed by Palace officials were long gone.

One event of the Thatcher years had a greater personal effect on the Queen than any other.

ABOVE The Queen and US President Ronald Reagan relaxing on horseback at Windsor, 1982.

RIGHT Sandringham, 1988: the Queen and Prince Philip with Charles and Diana, their sons William and Harry, and Anne's children Zara and Peter Phillips.

In 1982, Argentina invaded the Falkland Islands and Britain sent a task force on the long journey over the Atlantic to reclaim them. Prince Andrew, then a 22-year-old Royal Navy helicopter pilot, was aboard the aircraft carrier HMS *Invincible*. Some in the government felt he should not go, but a statement issued from Buckingham Palace made the Queen's position clear: "Prince Andrew is a serving officer and there is no question in her mind that he should go." The Prince flew missions that included using his Sea King helicopter as a decoy for Argentinian Exocet missiles as well as anti-submarine warfare, search-and-rescue and casualty evacuation.

The media's interest in Andrew did not end with the Falklands campaign, but turned from his wartime bravado to his private life, which

many found equally colourful. Among his childhood friends was Sarah Ferguson, daughter of the Major Ronald Ferguson, polo manager to first Prince Philip and later the Prince of Wales. Andrew and Sarah met again at Royal Ascot in 1985 and a year later they married at Westminster Abbey. The Duchess of York, or "Fergie" as she was known, was perceived as injecting new blood into the royal family: she was flamboyant, relaxed and popular.

If the marriages of Charles and Andrew were to cause increasing pain to the Queen, they were to give great pleasure, too, in the shape of four grandchildren. Princess Anne had given birth to her second child, Zara, in 1981, and the following year the Princess of Wales had her first son, William Arthur Philip Louis, second in line to the throne and a prince who would develop his own rapport with the public. Prince Harry was born to the Waleses two years later, and the Duke and Duchess of York also had two children, the Princesses Beatrice and Eugenie.

The business of royalty, of course, continued despite all the distractions that surrounded it. No head of state had travelled more than the Queen, and the 1980s witnessed more than 50 overseas tours to as many countries, some lasting several weeks. The highlight was perhaps the historic 1986 visit to China, the first by a British monarch. That tour is now best remembered for a light-hearted remark about "slitty eyes" made to a group of British students by the Duke of Edinburgh, but the visit was diplomatically significant, coming as it did at the beginning of negotiations between Britain and China over the transfer of Hong Kong. The Chinese rolled out the red carpet in the grandest possible way for the royal visitors and there is no doubt that the Queen won over the Chinese leader Deng Xiaoping. The then Foreign Secretary, Sir Geoffrey Howe, remembered one particular moment at a banquet given in honour of the royal visitors. Mr Deng, a chain smoker, was clearly uncomfortable and the Queen whispered to Sir Geoffrey, "I think Mr Deng would be happier if he was allowed to smoke."

OPPOSITE ABOVE Centre stage: Prince William steals the show at his brother Harry's christening in 1984.

OPPOSITE BELOW The Duke and Duchess of York and their daughter Beatrice with the Queen on the deck of the royal yacht *Britannia*, 1989.

ABOVE Roman Catholic nun and charity worker Mother Teresa of Calcutta receives the Order of Merit from the Queen in New Delhi, 1983.

As well as travelling, the Queen also played host to the two men responsible for momentous change in East–West relations during the 1980s. The first was American President Ronald Reagan, who stayed at Windsor Castle with his wife Nancy in 1982 and went riding with the Queen in Windsor Great Park. It was the first of three visits he was to make as President. In April 1989, the motorcade that swept up to Windsor Castle brought the Soviet leader Mikhail Gorbachev, the architect of reforms that made a new relationship with Britain and America possible. He and his wife Raisa were welcomed by the Queen and Prince Philip, and Mikhail Gorbachev was invited to inspect the Coldstream Guards. It would have been unthinkable a few years earlier.

As the Eighties wore on, though, media coverage of the personal lives of the royals became ever more febrile. Charles and Diana and, to a lesser extent Andrew and Sarah, were routine fodder for the tabloids. Both marriages were heading inexorably towards disaster, but there is little doubt that media pressure had some part to play in what happened. The Queen was preparing for the most difficult period of her long reign.

OPPOSITE A design for one of the Queen's dresses by Sir Hardy Amies which she wore during a State visit to the United States in 1983. Sir Hardy began designing for the Queen in 1950 and continued to do so until 1990, after which other designers working for the House of Hardy Amies continued to work for Her Majesty.

RIGHT The Queen and Prince Philip on the Great Wall of China at Badaling near Beijing, 1986.

Good Years and Bad

IN LATE NOVEMBER 1992, THE QUEEN WAS INVITED TO A LUNCHEON AT THE GUILDHALL IN THE CITY OF LONDON TO MARK THE FORTIETH ANNIVERSARY OF HER ACCESSION TO THE THRONE. THE INCLUSION OF ONE LATIN PHRASE IN THE SPEECH SHE GAVE THAT DAY CAME TO SYMBOLIZE THE MOST DIFFICULT PERIOD OF HER REIGN.

It would not, said the Queen, be a year on which she would look back with undiluted pleasure. In fact, it had turned out to be an "*annus horribilis*". And yet for all the headlines about "my horrible year", a later passage in that speech was much more significant.

Speculating on how future generations would judge events, the Queen suggested that history would take a "slightly more moderate view" than that of contemporary commentators who often lacked "moderation and compassion". And she went on: "No institution – city, monarchy or whatever – should expect to be free from the scrutiny of those who give it their loyalty and support, not to mention those who don't. But we are all part of the fabric of our national society and that scrutiny, by one part or another, can be just as effective if it is made with a touch of gentleness, good humour and understanding."

Given the caution with which royal addresses are finessed, this was very much a cry from the heart, for the Queen and members of her family now found themselves facing an almost relentless barrage of criticism. Stories of marriage difficulties were coupled with scathing commentaries on the behaviour of some of the younger royals, and accusations of profligacy inevitably included scrutiny of the royal finances.

For all the gathering storm clouds, the Queen began the 1990s with a notable diplomatic success. Shortly after Margaret Thatcher resigned to make way for John Major, Britain was involved in the first Gulf War, and when it was over the Queen travelled to Washington. In May 1991, she became the first British monarch to address a joint meeting of the US Congress and made an instant impact. Two days earlier, during the official welcoming ceremony on the White House lawn, the Queen had spoken from a podium embarrassingly adjusted so that only her hat was visible above the microphones. Now, on Capitol Hill, she began an historic speech by saying, "I do hope you can all see me today from where you are." It won a standing ovation and from then on was punctuated by bursts of applause.

Later that year, on the eve of her *annus horribilis*, the Queen used her Christmas broadcast to urge people to reflect "on our own good fortune" as the countries of Eastern Europe grappled with the challenges of their new-found freedom in the post-Soviet era. She had a promise for her subjects, too, to mark the first 40 years of her reign. "I feel the same

ABOVE Vice-President Dan Quayle and House Speaker Thomas Foley with the Queen before her address to the US Congress, 1991.

OPPOSITE *Annus horribilis*: Windsor Castle ablaze, November 1992.

obligation to you I felt in 1952," she said. "With your prayers and your help, and with the love and support of my family, I shall try to serve you in the years to come." It was seen by many as the Queen's response to growing speculation that she would consider standing down to make way for the Prince of Wales.

The omens of a difficult year came early in 1992. In February, the Queen and Prince Philip travelled to Australia to mark the 150th anniversary of the incorporation of the city of Sydney. The visit was overshadowed by coverage of the royal family's domestic difficulties, which seemed to have given added momentum to a

growing Australian republican movement. The country's Prime Minister, Paul Keating, had promised to make Australia a republic within a decade and his speech to welcome the Queen concentrated on links with regional neighbours rather than ties with Britain. The Queen did not return to Australia for eight years, heeding advice to stay away while the debate about her role as head of state continued. In the end, Australians voted in a 1999 referendum to maintain their ties to the British crown.

The marriages of the Queen's three eldest children unravelled with alarming speed and she seemed at times reduced to the role of

bewildered spectator. One of her long-standing companions, Lady Kennard, a godmother to Prince Andrew, reflected later: "The Queen would not have a row with anybody I don't think, but I think she was rather surprised at many things… the Queen, or anybody else, could never quite understand what Diana was about. I think it would be impossible."

For a time, it appeared that the difficulties of the Prince and Princess of Wales might be eclipsed by those of the Duke and Duchess of York, whose marital problems became increasingly public. If the former Sarah Ferguson had at first been welcomed as a breath of fresh

air within the royal family (and there is no doubt the Queen had considerable affection for her), her behaviour rapidly became a source of embarrassment. The couple's separation was announced by Buckingham Palace on 16 March, the day Parliament was dissolved for a general election. The first royal divorce happened the following month, when Princess Anne and Mark Phillips reached a settlement three years after their separation.

If the Yorks' parting of ways had at least been amicable, and the divorce of Princess Anne civilized, the rift between Charles and Diana became increasingly hostile. Their separation was finally announced in December, any lingering doubts about the gulf between them having been dispelled by recordings of telephone conversations between Diana and a friend, James Gilbey, and between Charles and Camilla Parker Bowles.

ABOVE A new stained-glass window installed after the Windsor Castle fire. The inclusion of scenes from the rescue operation at the castle was inspired by Prince Philip.

OPPOSITE Dressed in tartan: the Queen attends the Braemar Games in Scotland, 1994.

Good Years and Bad

Amid it all, on the morning of 20 November, a spotlight being used for renovation work in the Queen's private chapel at Windsor Castle set fire to a curtain. The flames spread rapidly, destroying nine of the castle's principal state rooms and damaging dozens of others. Prince Andrew was one of the first on the scene and helped carry works of art to safety. He described the Queen as "shocked and devastated", and a photograph of her surveying the wreckage captured her sense of utter desolation.

The years that followed were not that much better for the Queen than that dreadful *annus horribilis*. The separation of Charles and Diana simply served to trigger what the newspapers called "The War of the Waleses". It involved startling television interviews by both, in which adultery was admitted and old animosities made public. The prospect of divorce raised awkward constitutional questions, not least because the Prince of Wales would one day be head of a church that still refused to marry divorcés. Eventually, the Queen recognized that there was no alternative and told Charles and Diana their separation must become permanent. They were divorced in 1996, the same year as the Duke and Duchess of York.

The Princess of Wales was killed the following year, the victim of a car crash in Paris that also claimed the lives of her companion at the time, Dodi Fayed, and their driver, who was subsequently found to have been drinking. The Queen was at Balmoral at the time with the Duke of Edinburgh, the Prince of Wales and her two grandsons, William and Harry. It was five days before the royal family returned to London and the perceived insensitivity of the delay led to an unprecedented level of criticism of the Queen from both press and public. Her popularity was, briefly, under serious threat. She and Prince Philip left their car as it arrived at Buckingham Palace to look at the vast field of flowers that had

ABOVE Princess Anne and her second husband, Commander Timothy Laurence, are married at Balmoral, 1992.

RIGHT The Queen Mother wipes away a tear as her daughters join her to mark the fiftieth anniversary of VE Day (the end of the Second World War in Europe) in 1995.

been left there in Diana's memory. Many of the messages blamed the royal family for Diana's death and there is little doubt that until that moment the Queen had not grasped the depth of public grief.

That evening, the Queen made a live broadcast to the nation and finally expressed the sentiments so many had wanted to hear. She spoke from the heart, she said, as Queen and as a grandmother: "No one who knew Diana well will ever forget her. Millions of others, who never met her but felt they knew her, will remember her. I for one believe there are lessons to be drawn from her life and from the extraordinary and moving reaction to her death."

RIGHT Good neighbours: the Queen and French President François Mitterrand open the Channel Tunnel, 1994.

LEFT Field of flowers: the Queen and Prince Philip view the tributes to the late Diana, Princess of Wales, outside Buckingham Palace, September 1997.

BELOW The Queen and Prince Philip in a rare display of public affection at the Millennium Dome on New Year's Eve, 1999.

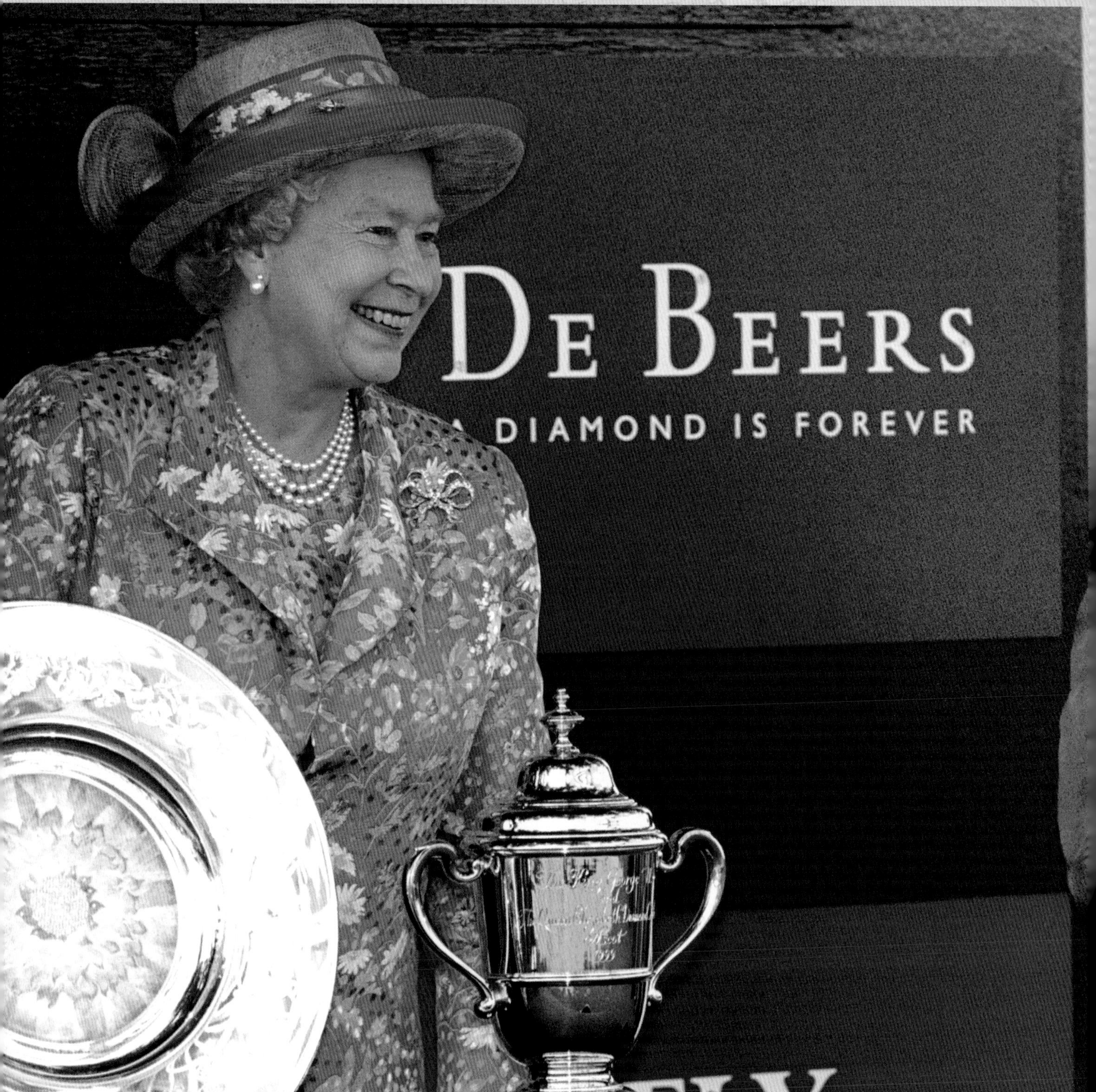
De Beers
A DIAMOND IS FOREVER

LEFT The Queen loves racing and she shares a joke with jockey Frankie Dettori at Royal Ascot, 1999.

BELOW Cheers: the Prince of Wales shares a joke with his mother at the celebrations to mark his fiftieth birthday in 1998.

Two months later the Queen again spoke in public, but at a very different occasion. Her Golden Wedding anniversary was celebrated with a lunch at London's Banqueting House and the Queen spoke glowingly of Prince Philip. "He is someone who doesn't take easily to compliments," she said, "but he has, quite simply, been my strength and stay all these years." But for all the air of celebration, Diana's death cast a shadow over the occasion and the Queen made what was interpreted as a promise to modernize the monarchy. Public opinion was often hard to read, she said, "but read it we must".

As the business of royalty carried on, with foreign tours and official visits up and down the United Kingdom, it became apparent that things were different, that the legacy of Diana had been felt at Buckingham Palace and Clarence House, home of the Prince of Wales. Royal events became a little less formal, the Queen more accessible. She was seen to be closer to ordinary people, visiting a pub, chatting to a pensioner at her flat in east London, mingling with crowds outside a Macdonald's drive-in. A new millennium, it seemed, was to herald happier times for the royal family.

The Golden Years

THE TURBULENCE OF THE EIGHTIES AND NINETIES WAS FOLLOWED BY SOME
WELCOME CALM FOR THE QUEEN AS THE NEW MILLENNIUM BEGAN. BY THE
TIME HER GOLDEN JUBILEE WAS CELEBRATED IN 2002 ELIZABETH WAS 76 YEARS
OLD, LONG PAST THE AGE OF RETIREMENT FOR MOST OF HER SUBJECTS, AND
YET SHE MAINTAINED A WORK SCHEDULE THAT BELIED HER YEARS.

Overseas tours became a little less frequent and not as lengthy as those during the early years of her reign, and yet in the first decade of the twenty-first century, she still made 23 trips abroad, visiting 26 countries, from Canada to the Vatican and from Latvia to Australia.

At home, meanwhile, there was no lessening of the pace. The Queen leads a comfortable, privileged life and is one of the richest women in the world, but she has a full-time job and works harder than any of her predecessors. It is not nine-to-five and it is not five days a week. The Queen devotes her mornings to paperwork and meetings, and there is an abundance of both. She receives more than 300 letters a day, reads a selection herself and decides how they are to be answered. Every day, home or abroad, she receives, and reviews, official

documents from government ministers and
Commonwealth officials. And almost every day
there are meetings and audiences that continue
throughout the morning.

Afternoons are set aside for public
engagements, and the Queen carries out
around 430 every year; some a short car
journey away, others involving much greater
distances. If she has used the royal train, she
will often spend the night on it. She frequently
hosts evening receptions at Buckingham
Palace or goes out to official dinners or
receptions. When Parliament is in session there
is a 7.30pm delivery containing a report of the
day's proceedings which the Queen will always
attempt to read that night. On Wednesday
evenings, she has her weekly audience with
the Prime Minister.

OPPOSITE Prince
Charles and the Queen
Mother at a pageant in
honour of her 100th
birthday in 2000.

ABOVE The family
portrait to mark the
marriage of Prince
Charles to Camilla
Parker Bowles, 2005.

RIGHT An audience
for the Queen with
Pope John Paul II at
the Vatican, 2000.

LEFT A nation mourns: the funeral of the Queen Mother at Westminster Abbey on 9 April 2002.

OPPOSITE The Queen celebrating her birthday in 2006. The cards give her age away!

One of the Queen's most important annual engagements is Holyroodhouse Week in Scotland, normally held in late June and early July. It begins with the Ceremony of the Keys, at which the Queen is formally welcomed back to Edinburgh. There is an investiture ceremony for Scottish residents recognized in the twice-yearly Honours List and Holyroodhouse is also the setting for the Queen's annual Scotland garden party. The weekly programme normally includes the Thistle Service at St Giles' Cathedral in Edinburgh. The Order of the Thistle is the highest honour in Scotland, awarded to men and women who have made an outstanding contribution to national life. It is second in precedence in the United Kingdom only to the Order of the Garter. There are just 24 Knights of the Garter, chosen personally by the Sovereign.

The Queen has made few concessions to age, but as the preparations for her Golden Jubilee were finalized in early 2002, she suffered the loss of two of those dearest to her. Her sister, Princess Margaret, died at the age of 71 on 9 February 2002. Princess Margaret had courted controversy for much of her life, not least over the breakdown of her marriage to the photographer Antony Armstrong-Jones, who became the Earl of Snowdon. The American author Gore Vidal, a personal friend, recalled that she once described herself as "the focus of the most creative malice, the evil sister".

In a cruel twist of irony, Princess Margaret had made her last public appearance the previous year at her mother's 101st birthday celebrations. And it was at Margaret's funeral that Queen Elizabeth the Queen Mother made her last public appearance before her own death six weeks later. For the Queen it was a time of intense personal grief. She had always maintained a loving relationship with her sister, and her mother had been a constant companion and source of great strength.

The Queen Mother died in her sleep in the Royal Lodge at Windsor with her daughter at her bedside. At the time, she was the longest-lived member of the British royal family in history, although her sister-in-law Princess Alice lived to be 102. The Queen Mother's body lay in state at Westminster Hall for three days and 200,000 people filed past the coffin. On the day of her funeral, crowds on the street were estimated at one million.

Personal tragedy was followed by public acclaim. Some in Britain had questioned what the public response to the Golden Jubilee celebrations would be, but when they began in the spring, the doubters were proved wrong. Hundreds of thousands of people turned out across the country as they had done for the Queen's Silver Jubilee in 1977. A "Prom at the

EℑR

A SERVICE

of

CELEBRATION

AND THANKSGIVING

ON THE OCCASION OF

THE GOLDEN JUBILEE

of

HER MAJESTY THE QUEEN

ST PAUL'S CATHEDRAL

Tuesday 4th June 2002

at 11.30 a.m.

ORDER OF SERVICE

At 10.25 a.m. the Dean and Chapter, the Bishop of London and the Archbishop of Canterbury leave the Dean's Aisle and proceed down the South Aisle to the Great West Door of the Cathedral.

At 10.30 a.m. Visiting Representatives of World Faiths leave the Minor Canons' Aisle and move to their places under the Dome.

At 10.30 a.m. the Choir of Her Majesty's Chapels Royal, the Choir of St Paul's Cathedral, the College of Minor Canons, Visiting Ecumenical Dignitaries, the Company of Honorary Canons, the College of Canons, Visiting Anglican Dignitaries, the Primus of the Episcopal Church of Scotland, the Archbishops of Wales and Armagh leave the Dean's Aisle and move to their places in Quire.

At 10.35 a.m. the Speaker, having been received by the Dean and Chapter, the Bishop of London and the Archbishop of Canterbury, leaves the West end of the Cathedral and moves in procession to his place under the Dome.

At 10.35 a.m. the Lord Chancellor, having been received by the Dean and Chapter, the Bishop of London and the Archbishop of Canterbury, leaves the West end of the Cathedral and moves in procession to his place under the Dome.

At 10.35 a.m. the Procession of the Orders of Chivalry leaves the Minor Canons' Aisle and proceeds down the North Aisle to the West end and the Centre Aisle to seats at the East end of the Nave.

From 10.35 a.m. Members of the Royal Family arrive by car and move in procession to their places under the Dome.

At 10.55 a.m. the Kings of Arms, Heralds and Pursuivants leave the Minor Canons' Aisle and proceed to the West end of the Cathedral.

From 11.10 a.m. Members of the Royal Family arrive by carriage at the foot of the steps and are conducted to the Great West Door.

At 11.20 a.m. the Lord Mayor arrives at the foot of the steps to await The Queen's arrival.

At 11.20 a.m. Members of the Royal Family move in procession through the Nave to their places under the Dome.

At 11.28 a.m. Her Majesty The Queen, His Royal Highness The Duke of Edinburgh, The Prince of Wales and The Princess Royal arrive at the foot of the steps and are conducted to the Great West Door. Her Majesty is preceded by the Lord Mayor bearing the Pearl Sword.

Her Majesty The Queen, His Royal Highness The Duke of Edinburgh, The Prince of Wales and The Princess Royal are received by the Dean and Chapter, the Bishop of London and the Archbishop of Canterbury and a procession is formed.

A fanfare is sounded and all stand.

5

INTROIT

I WAS glad when they said unto me: we will go into the house of the Lord.
Our feet shall stand in thy gates: O Jerusalem.
Jerusalem is builded as a city: that is at unity in itself.
Vivat Regina Elizabetha!
O pray for the peace of Jerusalem: they shall prosper that love thee.
Peace be within thy walls: and plenteousness within thy palaces.

Words Psalm 122. 1-3, 6, 7   *Music* CHARLES HUBERT HASTINGS PARRY
1848-1918
Arranged RICHARD BARNES b.1947

Remain standing as THE DEAN *gives*

THE BIDDING

WE come to this Cathedral Church to give thanks to Almighty God for the long reign of Her Majesty The Queen and to rejoice together at this time in her Golden Jubilee.

We come from all parts of this Realm and Commonwealth of Nations to celebrate our traditions of faith, of liberty, of law, of government, of public service, of compassion.

We come from many traditions of faith to pray for the wellbeing of all people; for the peace of the world; for the unity and prosperity of our nation; for the life of the Commonwealth; and for ourselves that we may do justly and love mercy and walk humbly with our God.

And we hold before God in prayer our Sovereign Lady The Queen; His Royal Highness The Prince Philip, Duke of Edinburgh; all members of the Royal Family; and we ask that throughout their lives they may be sustained and renewed by the power of God's Holy Spirit.

O God, who providest for thy people by thy power, and rulest over them in love: vouchsafe so to bless thy Servant Elizabeth our Queen, that under her this realm may be wisely governed, and thy Church may serve thee in all godly quietness; and grant that she, being devoted to thee with her whole heart, and persevering in good works unto the end, may, by thy guidance, come to thine everlasting kingdom; through Jesus Christ thy Son our Lord, who liveth and reigneth with thee and the Holy Spirit, ever one God, world without end. **Amen.**

6

NATIONAL ANTHEM

GOD save our gracious Queen,
Long live our noble Queen,
God save The Queen!
Send her victorious,
Happy and glorious,
Long to reign over us,
God save The Queen!

Thy choicest gifts in store
On her be pleased to pour,
Long may she reign:
May she defend our laws,
and ever give us cause
to sing with heart and voice
God save The Queen!

Words Traditional   *Music arranged* GORDON JACOB 1895-1984

Organ Voluntary:
Pomp and Circumstance March No. 4 *(arr. Hesford)* .. .. .. *Sir Edward Elgar*
1857-1934

17

BELOW Fireworks light the night sky over Buckingham Palace to mark the Queen's Golden Jubilee, 2002.

OPPOSITE An extract of pages from the Order of Service for the Queen's Golden Jubilee National Service of Thanksgiving on 4 June 2002 at St Paul's Cathedral. Speaking at a luncheon held at the Guildhall afterwards, the Queen said, "Gratitude, respect and pride, these words sum up how I feel about the people of this country and the Commonwealth – and what this Golden Jubilee means to me."

Palace" concert in the gardens of Buckingham Palace attracted two million applications for just 12,500 tickets. Three days later, a million people packed the streets of London for a jubilee procession to a service of thanksgiving at St Paul's Cathedral. The Queen travelled in a gold coach and every member of the royal family was present. In a speech at the Guildhall, the Queen captured the mood. "It has", she said, "been a pretty remarkable 50 years by any standards." There had been ups and downs, "but", she continued, "anyone who

can remember what things were like after those long six years of war appreciates what immense changes have been achieved since then."

During that Golden Jubilee year, the Queen and Prince Philip journeyed an estimated 40,000 miles across Britain and the world. Their travels began in Jamaica and went on to include New Zealand, Australia and Canada. There were tributes in non-Commonwealth countries, too. In New York, the top of the Empire State Building was illuminated in purple and gold, the royal colours. When it was

all over, the monarchy was felt to have repaired much of the damage caused by the scandals of earlier years. According to the ever-patriotic *Daily Mail*, "Britain was discovering the land of hope and glory."

Three years later, in 2005, the royal family took another major step in putting those scandals behind it. In the immediate aftermath of Diana's death the Prince of Wales had maintained a discreet relationship with Camilla Parker Bowles, the woman who had been the one true love of his life. But gradually Mrs Parker Bowles adopted a higher public profile and appeared to win increasing acceptance from both public and press, the latter chastened and more circumspect in the post-Diana era. The acceptance of Mrs Parker Bowles by William and Harry, who spoke glowingly of their father's devotion to them, played no small part in this.

On 10 February that year Buckingham Palace announced the couple's engagement. Plans began for another royal wedding, but an event strikingly different from that extraordinary day at St Paul's Cathedral 14 years earlier. The date for a civil ceremony at Windsor Castle was set for 8 April, but it was not that simple. First, embarrassed officials discovered that if the castle was used for one civil ceremony, it would, under law, have to be made available for others for the following year. On 4 April it was announced that the marriage would take place at the Guildhall in Windsor. However, Pope John Paul II died on 2 April and after it was revealed that arrangements meant his funeral service would take place on the 8th, the wedding was postponed by one day to allow the Prince of Wales to attend the Pope's requiem mass in St Peter's Square and then return for his wedding.

Charles and Camilla, both divorcés, were married at Windsor Guildhall on 9 April in front of just 30 family and friends. Prince William and Prince Harry were witnesses, along with Mrs Parker Bowles's own children. The Queen and Prince Philip did not attend,

although they attended the service of blessing in St George's Chapel and later a reception in Windsor Castle. The Queen gave Mrs Parker Bowles the title Her Royal Highness The Duchess of Cornwall and bestowed on her the position of second in the official order of preference for female royals at state occasions. She was, however, placed behind Princess Anne and Princess Alexandra at private functions. Some family sensibilities remained.

Within the House of Windsor there seemed to be peace at last. And more. For as William and Harry began to build their adult lives, the future appeared ever more promising.

William, third in line to the throne, had taken up his place at St Andrew's University in Scotland in 2001. It was there that he struck up a relationship with a fellow student, Catherine Middleton. The relationship was allowed to flourish largely unhindered by media intrusion after an agreement was struck between palace and press. There was to be none of the whirlwind pace of his parents' engagement and marriage, for William had learned painful lessons. His military career began in 2005 and he took on a greater number of royal duties. It was clear he had inherited his mother's charisma.

BELOW The State Opening of the Scottish Parliament, with First Minister Alex Salmond, 30 June 2007.

OPPOSITE "The waging of peace is the hardest form of leadership." The Queen addresses the United Nations, 6 July 2010.

The overwhelming proof of that came at the beginning of 2010 when, for the first time, Prince William formally represented the Queen on an overseas tour. He travelled first to New Zealand and then Australia, and his impact was immediate and overwhelming. Outside the new Supreme Court building in the New Zealand capital Wellington, William spent 45 minutes working the crowd. He fielded questions about his plans to marry Kate, admired photographs of his mother and chatted with an easy charm. At home in England, the Queen must have been watching with growing satisfaction.

Elizabeth herself had made no small impact overseas. At the end of her 2009 tour of Canada she stopped for a few short hours in New York. In 1957, she had addressed the United Nations as Britain's new, young Queen. Now, 53 years later, she returned with a message that was based on those years of experience. "It has perhaps always been the case that the waging of peace is the hardest form of leadership of all," she said. "I know of no single formula for success, but over the years I have observed that some attributes of leadership are universal, and are often about ways of encouraging people to combine their efforts, their talents, their insights, their enthusiasm and their inspiration to work together." She went on to visit Ground Zero and to lay a wreath in memory of British citizens killed in the attack on the twin towers in 2001.

The Queen, approaching her eighty-fifth birthday in 2011, had reason to be proud of her own style of leadership. If her popularity had seldom been under serious threat, the standing of the monarchy as an institution had faced some grave challenges. She had steered it into calmer waters and there were still notable triumphs to come.

Dinner

in honor of

Her Majesty Queen Elizabeth II

and *His Royal Highness The Prince Philip*

Duke of Edinburgh

Spring Pea Soup with Fernleaf Lavender

Chive Pizzelle with American Caviar

NEWTON CHARDONNAY "UNFILTERED" 2004

Dover Sole Almondine

Roasted Artichokes, Pequillo Peppers and Olives

Saddle of Spring Lamb

Chanterelle Sauce

Fricassee of Baby Vegetables

PETER MICHAEL "LES PAVOTS" 2003

Arugula, Savannah Mustard

and Mint Romaine

Champagne Dressing · Trio of Farmhouse Cheeses

"Rose Blossoms"

SCHRAMSBERG BRUT ROSÉ 2004

The White House   *Monday, May 7, 2007*

LEFT The Order of the Garter
service at Windsor, in 2008.
Prince William was installed
as the 1000th knight.

ABOVE A menu given for a dinner at the White
House in Washington DC that was held by
President and Mrs Bush in honour of the Queen's
State visit to the United States in 2007.

A Diamond Jubilee

IF 1992 HAD BEEN AN "ANNUS HORRIBILIS" FOR THE QUEEN, 2011 WAS
TO BECOME WHAT MANY COMMENTATORS LIKED TO CALL HER "ANNUS
MIRABILIS". IT WAS A PERFECT PRELUDE TO THE THE FOLLOWING YEAR'S
DIAMOND JUBILEE. THERE MIGHT HAVE BEEN DOUBTS ABOUT THE ROYAL
FAMILY'S ABILITY TO DRAW A CROWD, FEARS THAT TWENTY-FIRST-CENTURY
BRITAIN WAS MORE CYNICAL ABOUT THE PANOPLY OF MONARCHY, BUT ON
A SPRING MORNING IN LONDON SUCH MISGIVINGS WERE DISPELLED. AS
THEY HAD FOR HIS PARENTS 30 YEARS EARLIER, PEOPLE LINED THE STREETS
IN THEIR HUNDREDS OF THOUSANDS FOR THE WEDDING OF PRINCE
WILLIAM. OUTSIDE BUCKINGHAM PALACE AND WESTMINSTER ABBEY,
WHERE THE CEREMONY WAS CONDUCTED, BROADCASTERS FROM NEARLY
100 COUNTRIES AROUND THE WORLD TOLD THE STORY OF THE LATEST
ROYAL ROMANCE TO AN AUDIENCE IN EXCESS OF ONE BILLION.

Catherine Middleton appeared in a stunning wedding dress to captivate that audience, but she delivered a more significant message. Her demeanour, and that of Prince William, left no doubt that this was a young, modern couple genuinely in love. For observers, it was hard not to feel that the future of the monarchy was in safe hands.

The confetti had barely been swept away from the courtyard at Buckingham Palace before the Queen was setting off on one of the most important visits of her reign. No British

RIGHT Young and old alike flinch at a noisy fly-past on the Buckingham Palace balcony after the wedding of William and Kate, 29 April 2011. The children who made up the bride's troupe of bridesmaids and pageboys were (from left to right): Eliza Lopes, Lady Louise Windsor, Margarita Armstrong-Jones, Grace Van Cutsem, Tom Pettifer and Billy Lowther-Pinkerton.

....

ABOVE A toast at Buckingham Palace with visiting US President Barack Obama, 24 May 2011.

LEFT Another royal wedding: Zara Phillips and rugby player Mike Tindall in Edinburgh, July 2011.

monarch had set foot in Dublin for 100 years and such were the sensitivities involved that the Queen's visit had been a decade in the planning.

On 17 May, the Queen, dressed in the emerald green of Ireland, set foot on the tarmac at Casement Aerodrome, named after a man executed for treason after the 1916 uprising against British rule. The Queen laid a wreath at the Garden of Remembrance, which commemorates the men and women killed fighting for independence from the British crown, and the band played "God Save the Queen". It would have been unthinkable not long ago. She went on to visit Crome Park,

where British troops and police had shot dead 14 people at a Gaelic football match during Ireland's War of Independence in 1920, and that evening, at a state banquet, the Queen extended her sympathy to all those who had suffered in a troubled past. "With the benefit of historical hindsight," she said, "we can all see things which we wish had been done differently or not at all."

The Queen does not enter political debate, but her visit to Ireland did more to overcome decades of hostility and suspicion than any politician could have achieved. There were some protests, small and noisy, but when the Queen flew home from Cork, once a stronghold of

the republican movement, she left behind a nation that had extended to her the warmest of welcomes. The past was not forgotten, but old animosities were being left behind.

Later in the year she was to travel further afield on perhaps the last of her major, long distance overseas tours. It was widely described as the Queen's farewell to Australia, a description first used by a palace official who later backtracked. Last visit or not, it was the Queen's sixteenth and the crowds seemed as big as ever. In Brisbane, ravaged by floods earlier in the year, thousands of people lined the river bank to cheer on the British monarch.

ABOVE Talking to actress Dame Judi Dench and sculptor Anish Kapoor during a reception at Buckingham Palace for the Praemium Imperiale Awards, July 2011.

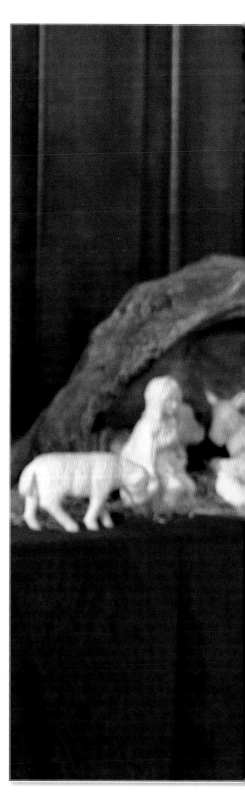

LEFT *Annus mirabalis*: the Queen at the English market in Cork during her historic visit to Ireland, June 2011.

RIGHT Queen Elizabeth II at Hampton Court Palace for the recording of her Christmas broadcast in 2010.

"We have been overwhelmed by your kindness and support," the Queen told well-wishers in Perth, the last stop on her Australian journey. It was here that Commonwealth leaders had gathered for their biennial heads of government meeting. Their order of business included changes to Britain's rules of royal succession. They have now ended bias in favour of male descendants of the sovereign and removed the ban on heirs to the throne marrying Roman Catholics.

If there was a cloud in the bright, new sky above the House of Windsor, it came in the form of concerns about the health of the Duke of Edinburgh. As the Queen and her family prepared for their annual Christmas celebrations at Sandringham at the end of 2011, Prince Philip was taken to hospital in Cambridge suffering from chest pains. He was treated for a blocked coronary artery and kept in hospital for five days. The Queen went to visit on Christmas Eve and the Prince's six adult grandchildren on Christmas Day. When Philip was driven back to Sandringham two days later, he gave a cheery wave and appeared, in the words of one newspaper, "whip crack smart". But as the Diamond Jubilee got underway, there were to be more visits to hospital and more worries about his health.

Only one other British monarch has celebrated a Diamond Jubilee. Queen Victoria reached her 60 years on the throne on 22 June 1897. Then there was some argument about how extensive the celebrations should be and who should pay. In the event the 78-year-old Queen, dressed in black as she had been since her beloved Prince Albert's death 36 years earlier, set off on a triumphant six-mile carriage procession through the streets of London. In the capital, and in Manchester, hundreds of thousands of the poorest residents were given "street feasts" with free beer and tobacco. Britain was at the height of its power and Victoria ruled over an empire of 450 million people around the globe. She was not given to false modesty, and wrote of the Jubilee: "No one, I believe, has met with such an ovation as was given to me."

A Diamond Jubilee

The anniversary of Victoria's accession to the throne fell on a summer's day, and in 1897 the June weather was particularly pleasant. By contrast, her great-great-granddaughter Elizabeth became Queen in February, a chilly time of year for processions and street parties and the Queen dislikes celebrations marking the day her father had died at the age of just 56.

So, like Victoria before her, the Queen marked her Diamond Jubilee in June, over one long weekend that, once again, saw supporters of the monarchy turn out in great numbers. At its heart was the river pageant on the Thames, an event inspired by a painting by Canaletto of the extravagant waterborne procession for The Lord Mayor of London in 1750.

The 2012 version may have been rather more strictly controlled than Canaletto's – health and safety was not a priority in the eighteenth century, after all – but it was nevertheless a masterpiece in its own right. One thousand vessels of all shapes, sizes and ages made their way up the Thames to Tower Bridge in a procession that stretched back over seven-and-a-half miles and took 90 minutes to pass any given point. At its head was the *Gloriana*, a barge powered by 18 oarsmen, including Olympians Sir Steven Redgrave and Sir Matthew Pinsent.

Much attention inevitably focused on the flotilla of Dunkirk "little ships" used in the evacuation of British troops in 1940. Aboard one was Vic Viner, 95 years old and believed to be the only survivor of the Royal Navy operation at Dunkirk. "I never expected in my lifetime to be doing this," he said. "Not in my wildest dreams."

The royal party arrived at Tower Bridge in pouring rain to the strains of "Land of Hope and Glory" from the chamber choir of the Royal College of Music. And when the London Philharmonic Orchestra struck up the hornpipe there was the faintest suggestion of regal bobbing up and down. The following day Prince Philip was taken to hospital with a urinary infection.

There were some suggestions that the Duke of Edinburgh might not have been too sorry to miss the Jubilee concert on the Mall in front of Buckingham Palace, even though the Prince of Wales told the crowd "if we shout loud enough he might just hear us." It was a night when Charles declared: "Mummy, thanks for making us proud to be British" and Stevie Wonder sang a version of "Isn't She Lovely" re-written for the occasion.

But the Queen lit the first of thousands of Jubilee beacons without her constant companion at her side and the following day travelled to St Paul's cathedral not with her husband but a lady-in-waiting. The Queen's solitary progress up the steps of the cathedral remains one of the abiding images of four days of so much celebration. She was not alone on the balcony of Buckingham Palace later to greet the crowd. But the presence at her side of only Prince Charles and Prince William, their wives and Prince Harry was widely interpreted as a statement about core values replacing extravagance. Or as one commentator put it: "an exercise in brand management".

There were many superlatives over that Diamond Jubilee weekend. In my own coverage I wrote about "a tide of devotion" carrying the monarch along the Thames. But perhaps the occasion was best captured by the words of one young woman. She was standing among the crowds in a riverside park and soaked to the skin. "It's been a fantastic day, a great day," she said. "We saw the Queen. We laughed, we danced, we sang with people, we waved our flags. It's what we wanted."

....

RIGHT A tribute on the Thames. The flotilla approaches Tower Bridge in the river pageant to mark the Queen's Diamond Jubilee in June, 2012.

OVERLEAF The royal family gathers at Buckingham Palace after Trooping the Colour in the Diamond Jubilee year, 2012. A family now at peace with itself.

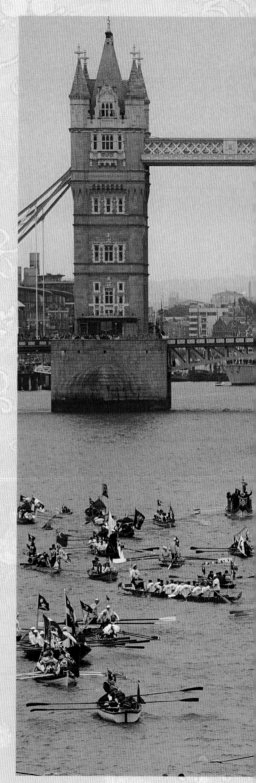

An Expanding Family

SOUTH WHARF ROAD BEHIND PADDINGTON STATION IS AN UNREMARKABLE LONDON STREET, BUT EVERY NOW AND THEN IT BECOMES THE SETTING FOR AN EXTRAORDINARY MEDIA FRENZY. FOR THIS IS THE HOME OF THE LINDO WING, THE PRIVATE SECTION OF ST. MARY'S HOSPITAL AND THE MATERNITY UNIT FAVOURED BY ROYALTY. FOUR OF THE QUEEN'S EIGHT GRANDCHILDREN WERE BORN HERE AND IT WAS ON THE STEPS OF THE LINDO THAT PRINCE CHARLES AND DIANA PRINCESS OF WALES PRESENTED FIRST PRINCE WILLIAM AND THEN PRINCE HARRY TO THE WORLD.

The scenes then were chaotic enough, but South Wharf Road was a sea of calm compared to what was to follow in July 2013. A very different and much bigger media circus was in town to await the birth of George Alexander Louis, Prince of Cambridge and future King of the United Kingdom.

The Queen, of course, was already a great grandmother by the time George arrived. Her grandson Peter Phillips and his Canadian wife Autumn had two daughters: Savannah, born at the end of 2010, and Isla, a Diamond Jubilee baby delivered in March 2012. The children of Princess Anne, Peter and his sister Zara, have no royal titles and none were bestowed on their children.

Zara, an Olympic silver medallist as a member of Great Britain's 2012 equestrian team, is married to the former England rugby international Mike Tindall. Their wedding reflected their lifestyle. It was far from the traditional royal occasion, despite the presence of the Queen and Prince Philip. The groom chewed gum as he waited for a bride who has kept her own name professionally and is otherwise known simply Mrs Tindall. Their daughter, Mia, was born at an NHS hospital in Gloucestershire on what her father described as "the best day of my life". Mike Tindall has the familiar look of a rugby player who's been in the sporting wars, and Zara's brother Peter Phillips joked about Mia. "She's very pretty," he told reporters. "She certainly doesn't have Mike's nose if that's what you're asking."

If the Tindall and Phillips children were born and introduced to the world without fuss, the same cannot be said of the Cambridges. The arrival of Prince George, and later Princess Charlotte, was accompanied by royal fanfare at its loudest.

In South Wharf Road during that hot July in 2013, the camera operators and the photographers began to gather long before the big day. The first to arrive, an American

ABOVE A great-grandmother: the christening of Savannah Phillips at Avening, Gloucestershire, 2011.

OPPOSITE Born to be king. Prince George of Cambridge, third in line to the throne, is presented to the world as he is taken home from St. Mary's Hospital, Paddington, the day after his birth in July 2013.

television news team, checked into their hotel a full three weeks before Prince George was born and began to mount a daily vigil. Another team, from a TV news agency, offered 24-hour, uninterrupted live pictures of the front door of the Lindo Wing. The *Sun* newspaper streamed it on their website, immediately attracting a vociferous rant from campaigners opposed to their Page Three pictures.

London taxi drivers began to refer to South Wharf Road as Crazy Street and there was indeed an air of madness about the place. The pavement opposite the Lindo wing was marked out in tape by television crews reserving a space. British and US broadcasters seized the prime spots and stretching for nearly 100 yards were the spaces for teams from across Europe, Asia and Australia. The photographers' pens were a forest of aluminium step ladders, left in place ahead of the day when the "snappers" would unleash a barrage of motor driven cameras in search of the one perfect shot. In the absence of news, television correspondents interviewed each other. "Why is this so important to Britain?" a Chinese reporter asked me. "Why is it so interesting in China?" I asked her when we changed places.

The answer, of course, is that the world is as fascinated by a British royal baby as it is by a royal wedding. It is the monarchy as fairytale. A happy ending in an all too often gloomy world. Graham Smith, who runs the anti-monarchy group Republic, made himself available to express an alternative view to journalists outside the Lindo. The vast majority of British people, he said, simply wanted to get on with their lives and in times of economic difficulty had little interest in a new member of such a privileged family.

LEFT The royal wave. Prince George front and centre on the balcony at Buckingham Palace after Trooping the Colour in June 2015.

OPPOSITE Now we are four. The Duke and Duchess of Cambridge with the newborn Princess Charlotte at St. Mary's Hospital on 2 May 2015.

RIGHT Princess Charlotte Elizabeth Diana, just two months old, at her christening at Sandringham in July 2015. She is fourth in line to the throne.

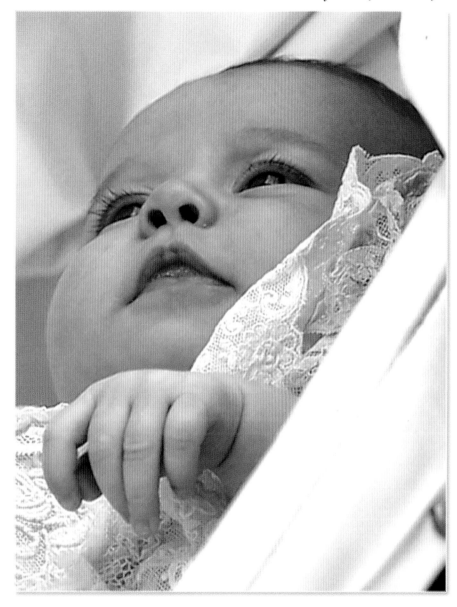

Prince George was born just before 4.30 in the afternoon on Monday, 22 July. He weighed 8lb 6oz, a healthy boy with, in the words of his father, "a good pair of lungs on him". For the vast throng of media outside the wait was over. The only question: would the proud parents provide some good pictures and, as a bonus, a few words?

William and Kate did not disappoint. The Duke of Cambridge may have grown up with a dislike of the media, but he understands their fascination with his family and the need, every now and then, to satisfy their insatiable appetite.

The royal couple stood for pictures on the steps of the Lindo wing and then walked to the microphones. "Very emotional," said Kate. "He's a big boy. He's quite heavy," said William. "He's got more hair than me, thank God."

An Expanding Family

The Queen had not been among visitors to the hospital, but she was driven to William and Kate's home at Kensington Palace shortly after they arrived back there. An official statement had spoken of her delight at the birth of another great-grandchild and a few months after her Diamond Jubilee she was able to reflect on a surge of popularity for the House of Windsor as its younger members began to take centre stage.

During the Jubilee, the Queen and Prince Philip had toured all parts of the United Kingdom, but not ventured further afield. Overseas travels were shared among other members of the royal family, with one particularly striking success.

Prince Harry made his debut as the Queen's representative abroad in the Caribbean, travelling first to Belize and then Jamaica. Before he arrived, Jamaica's Prime Minister Portia Simpson Miller had reiterated her call for full independence, with the British monarch removed as head of state. Harry may not have changed the political debate, but his embrace of a beaming Mrs Simpson Miller certainly set the tone for a tour that went some way towards winning friends and influencing people.

Harry raced and joked with Jamaican sprinter Usain Bolt, the world's fastest man, and danced in Trenchtown, where reggae was born and Bob Marley rose to fame. Marley's widow, Rita, gave Harry one her late husband's scarves. The *Jamaica Gleaner* newspaper described the royal visit as "pure laughter and fun". The Queen, we were told, was very pleased with her grandson.

The other high-profile Jubilee tour took William and Kate to Malaysia, Singapore, the Solomon Islands and the remote island of Tuvalu in the south Pacific. It was soured by controversy over the publication in France of photographs of the Duchess topless during a holiday in Provence. The paparazzi intruded into the couple's private life and protests and threats of legal action by palace officials were

to have little effect on events still to come.

But if a shadow had fallen over that tour in 2012, the sun could not have shone more brightly when William and Kate headed for New Zealand and Australia to years later with Prince George, just nine months old when they embarked on the long flight to the New Zealand capital Wellington.

It is no small achievement to steal the limelight from the Duchess of Cambridge. She was photographed hitting a cricket ball, sailing a racing yacht and, amid unfounded rumours that she was again pregnant, sipping wine at a vineyard. It was a long tour and Prince George made just two official public appearances. But he was the person the public and the media wanted to see. Excited Australian commentators talked of this one small boy setting back by years the cause of republicanism.

Media access to the new royal star was strictly controlled. When Charles and Diana had introduced Prince William to New Zealand on the lawn of Wellington's government house in 1983, scores of photographers lined up to capture the moment. Thirty-one years later, as George played with other toddlers at a party in the same house, just two were allowed inside to take pictures to be shared among all the others.

And of course, as the Queen and Prince Philip watched it all unfolding on their television screens, their family was not yet complete. Kate was not pregnant in New Zealand despite all the speculation, but on 8 September 2014, just five months after that triumphant tour with Prince George, it was announced that she was expecting a second baby.

....

RIGHT A day out to watch the polo. The Duchess of Cambridge and an 11 month old Prince George at the Beaufort Polo Club, Gloucestershire. June, 2014.

An Expanding Family

And so it was that the media circus moved back to South Wharf Road and the Lindo Wing. Better organized than for Prince George, perhaps, but none the less enthusiastic. Bookmakers did a brisk trade accepting bets on the gender and name of the new baby – Alice was the favourite choice – and Britain's obsession with the May general election was briefly put on hold.

Charlotte Elizabeth Diana, Princess of Cambridge, was born early in the morning of Saturday, 2 May, just five days before the election. She is fourth in line to the throne. After changes to the rules of succession, it is a position she will not have to surrender to any younger brothers. Barely 10 hours after being admitted to hospital, Kate and William took their new daughter home. They were anxious to keep disruption to hospital routine to a minimum.

Prince George had been baptized very privately in the Chapel Royal at St. James's Palace. His sister's christening was a public affair. It took place at St. Mary Magdalene Church on the Queen's Sandringham estate and people were invited to line the route as members of the royal family walked to the church. Kate pushed Charlotte in a pram, Prince George walked hand in hand with his father. Now they were four.

The Queen must have surveyed the scene with considerable satisfaction. This was a happy family, its future in safe hands. She could prepare for some more significant milestones of her own, content that the turbulence that had once so unsettled the House of Windsor was very much in the past.

....

RIGHT A salute for a new royal baby. The Duke and Duchess of Cambridge with Prince George take Princess Charlotte to be christened at Sandringham, July 2015.

Long to Reign Over Us

When Queen Victoria died on the Isle of Wight on a January evening in 1901, she had been on the throne for 63 years and 216 days, Britain's longest-reigning monarch by a margin of more than four years. Victoria was just 18 when she became Queen and as her reign ended it must have seemed unlikely that any monarch could exceed the extraordinary length of her time on the throne.

Her great-great-granddaughter did so on 9 September 2015, at around 5.30 in the afternoon according to those who had literally counted the hours. Elizabeth II wanted no fuss; she dislikes celebrating anniversaries associated with the deaths of her predecessors. Initially, it seemed there would be no engagements in the royal diary at all for that day, that the Queen would remain out of sight on the Balmoral estate where she spends her summer holidays.

In the event, there was a great deal of fuss. Bells rang out at cathedrals across the country and special services were held. Thirty minutes were set aside in the House of Commons for tributes led by Prime Minister David Cameron, who said she had been "a golden thread running through three postwar generations". The Royal Mint struck a commemorative coin, there was a river pageant on the Thames and even the

odd street party. And, of course, the person at the centre of it all emerged in public, now sending the message "business as usual".

The royal engagement on this momentous day appeared, on the surface, routine: the re-opening after 56 years of the railway line from Edinburgh to the Scottish borders. Inevitably, it was anything but routine as the day unfolded on live television. The Queen boarded a train pulled by the Union of South Africa, a magnificent steam engine built in 1937. As it puffed through the Scottish countryside, cheering crowds lined the route and a TV helicopter hovered overhead.

The Queen's response to all this was predictably modest, although it seemed she was not unhappy with the ballyhoo. She insisted that the longest reign was not something to which she had ever aspired. "Inevitably a long life can pass by many milestones; mine is no exception," she said. "I thank you all, and the

many others at home and overseas, for your touching messages of great kindness."

The Queen might have preferred no fuss over the longest reign, but the same could not be said for events that marked her 90th birthday, some seven months later. The Queen has two birthdays, of course. The official version is usually celebrated on the second Saturday in June, a day when it was believed the weather would be more reliable for the Trooping the Colour parade and a royal appearance on the balcony of Buckingham palace.

The Queen's actual birthday is April 21st and as she turned 90 in 2016 she set off with Prince Philip on yet another royal walkabout. The route was not long, from the gates of Windsor Castle and around the corner to the Guildhall. But the crowds were huge and the reception rapturous. At the Guildhall there was a birthday cake and a welcome from other 90-year-olds, and then the Queen and

RIGHT The Queen, with the Prince of Wales and the Duchess of Cornwall in Bayeux on the 70th anniversary of D-Day in June 2015.

OVERLEAF A somber moment. The Queen and Prince Philip honour those who died at the Bergen Belsen concentration camp on a visit to Germany in June 2015.

TO THE MEMORY OF ALL THOSE
WHO DIED IN THIS PLACE

the Duke boarded an open-topped Range Rover to be driven triumphantly through the streets of the town they regard as home.

That evening, in front of Windsor Castle, the Queen lit the first of 90 beacons stretching across the UK and overseas to mark the occasion. Prince Charles called for three cheers and told her: "I find it very hard to believe that you've reached your 90th year and I suddenly realised the other day that I have known you since you were 22 years old."

The Queen represents tradition and constancy, but she has also embraced change. On her birthday she sent a tweet. "I send my best wishes to those who are celebrating their 90th birthday," it said. "On this shared occasion I send my warmest congratulations to you."

As the Queen reached the landmark of the longest reign, the record showed she had made 261 official visits to 116 countries. Her later tours may not have lasted as long, nor covered the distance of some of those early royal journeys, but their impact has been none the less powerful.

In June 2014, the Queen joined world leaders in France to mark the 70th anniversary of the Normandy landings in the Second World War and to honour those who fell as the Allies began their final assault on Hitler's Germany. Peace and prosperity can never be taken for granted, she warned, and must be constantly tended so that "never again do we have cause to build monuments to our fallen youth".

The following year she travelled to Germany, staying at a hotel in the shadow

BELOW With Pope Francis at the Vatican in 2014. It was the Queen's fifth visit to meet a Pope in Rome.

OPPOSITE "Queen of the French." With President Francois Hollande and Mayor of Paris Anne Hidalgo at the flower market re-named in her honour, June, 2014.

MARCHÉ AUX FLEURS
REINE ELIZABETH II

of the Brandenburg Gate and standing in what was East Berlin before the Berlin Wall was torn down in 1989. At a state dinner she talked of the dangers of a divided Europe. "In our lives we have seen the worst but also the best of our continent," she said.

The Queen had not before visited the site of a Nazi concentration camp and her last stop in Germany was Bergen-Belsen, the camp in northern Germany liberated by British troops on 15 April 1945. The first Allied soldiers to arrive encountered appalling scenes and three veterans, along with camp survivors, were on hand to give the Queen a first-hand account. She walked with Prince Philip past the mass graves of Belsen, a place that epitomizes the worst of Europe.

There was, of course, light to go with the shade on these journeys. At the Vatican, the Queen had a first meeting with Pope Francis and was presented with a gift for Prince George – "the little boy" as the Pope described him. It was a blue orb with a silver cross. The Queen gave an obligatory response: "He'll be thrilled," she said, adding, after a moment's reflection: "When he's a little older."

In France, after the solemn D-Day commemorations, the Queen was thrilled to visit the historic flower market close to Notre Dame, and to find that it had been re-named in her honour as "Marché Aux Fleurs Reine Elizabeth II". This was the idea of the socialist Mayor of Paris Anne Hidalgo, who said it reflected the enormous affection in which Parisians hold the British Queen. The decision angered some of the Mayor's left-wing councillors, unhappy that such an honour should be bestowed on an unelected head of state by a country that had guillotined

....

RIGHT The Queen and Prince Philip are joined by Scotland's First Minister Nicola Sturgeon as they re-open a railway line to the Scottish Borders. On this day, 9 September 2015, the Queen becomes Britain's longest reigning monarch.

its own royal family at the end of the eighteenth century. To add to their irritation, the newspaper *Le Monde* declared her "The Queen of the French".

The Queen's Diamond Jubilee in 2012 had been a cause for several days of celebration, but her Sapphire Jubilee was very different. The Queen did not go out on 6 February 2017, and marked her 65 years on the throne in what was described as "quiet reflection." She was at Sandringham House in Norfolk, where her father George VI died in 1952.

For the Royal family, the year 2017 had a strong sense of transition. Prince Philip, at the age of 96, announced his retirement from public engagements, although he was still frequently seen at the Queen's side. The Duchess of Cambridge announced she was expecting another baby, a sixth great-grandchild for the Queen. And Prince Harry had an announcement too: his engagement to Meghan Markle, an American divorcee of mixed-race heritage. If ever evidence was needed of upheaval and change within the House of Windsor, it was this. Elizabeth II had succeeded her father to the throne only because her uncle, King Edward VIII, had been forced to abdicate to marry an American divorcee.

The Queen is often smothered in compliments, a tide of affection that gains strength on occasions like jubilees and birthdays. But it is praise from the least expected quarters that can be the most telling. Martin McGuinness is a former commander of the IRA, a republican who believes passionately in a united and independent Ireland. He first met the Queen, in his capacity as Northern Ireland's Deputy First Minister, during her Diamond Jubilee visit to Belfast. Their handshake was both historic and controversial. It was captured on camera, but no sound recording was allowed.

They met again two years later when the Queen went to Belfast's Crumlin Road jail, now a tourist attraction. Mr McGuinness and the then unionist First Minister Peter

Robinson were her guides. Both had been held at Crumlin Road during the Troubles in Northern Ireland. In a BBC documentary, Martin McGuinness paid a telling tribute to the Queen: "She knows my history. She knows I was a member of the IRA. She knows I was in conflict with her soldiers, yet both of us were prepared to rise above all of that. I liked her courage in agreeing to meet with me. I liked the engagements that I've had with her. There's nothing I have seen in my engagements with her that this is someone I should dislike. I like her."

It would, of course, be premature to start looking beyond Britain's longest-reigning monarch, to assume that her presence will somehow become diminished with her age. Prince Harry reflected on her extraordinary energy at the time of the Diamond Jubilee: "She smiles constantly. She's able to go into a room and bring the room to life. These are things that at her age she shouldn't be doing, and yet she's carrying on and doing them."

How best to summarize her reign? In 2014, during her visit to France, President François Hollande said she was the personification of the saying "Keep calm and carry on". Perhaps, though, the final word should belong to the Queen herself. In 1957, at the age of 31, she made her first televised Christmas broadcast and compared her role to that of monarchs in days gone by. She said: "I cannot lead you into battle, I do not give you laws or administer justice, but I can do something else, I can give you my heart and my devotion to these small islands and to all the peoples of our brotherhood of nations." Keeping that promise perhaps explains the enduring popularity of Elizabeth II.

LEFT Crowds gather outside Buckingham Palace for a light show during the "Party at the Palace", which was held as part of the celebrations that marked the Queen's Golden Jubilee in 2002.

Index

A
Aberfan disaster _51_
Aden 37
Alice, Princess 89
Amies, Hardy
  clothes designed by _61, 74_
Andrew, Prince 44, _45_, 46, _46, 54–5_, 80
  children _72_, 73
  divorce 80
  marriage _72_, 73, 75, 77–8
  naval career 67, 72
Anne, Princess 26, _28, 33, 48_, 53, _54–5_, 61
  attempted kidnap 58
  children 57, _60_, 73
  first marriage 57–8, _57_, 77, 78
  second marriage 80
  sporting career 58
annus horribilis 76–80
Armstrong-Jones, Antony _see_ Snowdon, Lord
Armstrong-Jones, Lady Sarah _57_
Australia 8, 29, 36, 37, 38, 40, 42, 56, 77, 91, 93, 99–100, 109, 112
  standard _36_

B
Balmoral _9_, 20, 53, _80_, 116
Banda, Hastings 45
Beaton, Cecil _31_
Beatrice, Princess _72_, 73
Belize 113
Belsen concentration camp 117, _118–19_
Benn, Tony 50
Bermuda 36, 37, _37_, 38
Bolt, Usain 112
Braemar Games 79
brand management 102
Brighton bomb 70
British Empire 36
broadcasts 52
  Children's Hour 16, 17–18, _17_, 20
  Christmas 30, 50, 52, 70, 76–7, _100–1_
  Commonwealth Day address 36, _44_
  coronation 30, _32_
  Elizabeth's wedding 25
  following death of Diana 81
  Royal Family documentary 52–3, _53, 54–5_
  William's wedding 96
Buckingham Palace 15, _82–3_, 87, _96–7_
  Belgian Suite 46
  Changing of the Guard 67
  garden parties 56, _58_, 70
  Party at the Palace 102, _124–5_
  Prom at the Palace 89, 91
  World War II 16

C
Burmese (horse) 66, _66_

C
Caernarfon Castle 52, _53_
Callaghan, James 61
Cambridge, Duchess of _see_ Middleton, Catherine
Cambridge, Duke of _see_ William, Prince
Canada 36, _38_, 91
  standard _36_
Casement Aerodrome 98
Ceremony of the Keys 89
Ceylon 36, 37
Chamberlain, Neville 16, 21
Channel Tunnel _81_
Chapel Royal 114
Charles, Prince _33, 48, 54–5_, 57, _86_
  birth 26, _27, 28, 29_
  childhood 26
  children _71_, 73
  divorce 80
  education 46
  fiftieth birthday celebrations 85
  first marriage 66–7, _68–9_, 70, _71_, 75, 77, 78
  Investiture 52, _53_
  and Mountbatten 59
  second marriage _87_, 92
Charlotte, Princess 106, _110, 111_, 113, 114, _114–15_
Children's Hour broadcast 16, _17_–18, _17_, 20
Churchill, Winston 10, 21, 28, 30, 46, 61
Clarence House 85
clothes 74
  coronation dress 30, _31_, 36
  Silver Jubilee outfit _61_
  wedding dress 22, 25, _25_
Coco Islands 37
Colville, Richard 52
Commonwealth 36–45, 70, 71, 87
  Commonwealth Day address 36, _44_
  realms 36
Commonwealth Games 36, 44
Cornwall, Duchess of _see_ Parker Bowles, Camilla
coronation 4, 30–2, _30–5_
  dress 30, _31_, 36
  oath of allegiance _32_
  Philip's act of homage 32
  procession 30, _33_
  television broadcast 30, _32_
Crawford, Marion "Crawfie" 10
  The Little Princesses 10
Crossman, Richard 47, 50
crown 30, _30, 31, 33_

D
Dench, Judi _99_
Deng Xiaoping 73
Dettori, Frankie _84–5_

Diamond Jubilee 4, 36, 40, 96, 100, 102, _102–3_, 113, 120, 124, 125
Douglas Home, Alec 46
Dunkirk evacuation 102

E
Eden, Anthony 46
Edinburgh, Duke of _see_ Philip, Prince
Edward, Prince 46, _46_, 53, _54–5_, 57
Edward VIII 6, 11, 20, 58
  abdication 11, _12_, 15, 21
  funeral 58
Eisenhower, Dwight D. _42_
Elizabeth II
  accession 28, _29_, 30, 102
  birth 6, _6_, 8
  childhood 6–15
  children 26, 44, 46, 53, _54–5_
  coronation _see_ coronation
  education 10, 15
  grandchildren 57, _60, 71, 72_, 73
  great-grandchildren 106–14
  marriage _see_ marriage
  temperament 10, 15
Elizabeth, Queen (Queen Mother) 6, _10, 14, 15, 18_, 26, _27_, 58, _60, 81_, 86
  death 89
  funeral _88_, 89
  World War II 16, 20
Eugenie, Princess 73

F
Facebook 4
Fagan, Michael 66
Falklands War 67, 72
Fayed, Dodi 80
Ferguson, Sarah _72_, 73, 75, 77–8, 80
Fiji 37
film premiers 59
Fisher, Archbishop Geoffrey 30
Flickr 4
Foley, Thomas 77
Francis, Pope _120_, 122

G
garden parties 56, _58_, 70, 89
George, Prince 106–14, _107, 108–09_, 109–10, _112–13, 114–15_, 124
  birth 106
George V 6, 8, _9_–10, _10_
  death 11
George VI 6, _6_, 10–11, _18_, 27
  accession _12–13_, 15
  coronation _14_, 15
  death 4, 26, 28, 30, 102
  stammer 11
Ghana 40, _41_, 44–5
Gibraltar 37
Gilbey, James 78
Girl Guides 21
Golden Jubilee 89, _90_, 91–2, _91_
Golden Wedding 85
Gorbachev, Mikhail 75
Gulf War, First 76

H
Harry, Prince _71_, 72, 73, 80, 92, 102, 106, 120, 125
  state visits 112
Hartnell, Norman
  Elizabeth's coronation dress 30, _31_, 36
  Elizabeth's wedding dress 22, 25, _25_
Heath, Edward 59, 61
Heseltine, William 52, 56
Hidalgo, Anne 124
Hillary, Edmund 30
Hollande, François _121_, 125
Holyroodhouse 56, 70, 89
Holyroodhouse Week 89
Honours List 89
horse racing _84–5_, 120
horses, love of 10, 120
Howe, Geoffrey 73
Hyde Park nail bomb 67

I
India _43_, 44, 73
investitures 89
Irish Republican Army (IRA) 59, 66–7, 70, 124
  bomb attacks 67, 70

J
Jamaica 36, 37, 91, 112
John Paul II, Pope 87, 92
Jubilee Walkway 57

K
Kapoor, Anish _99_
Kaunda, Kenneth 45
Keating, Paul 77
Kennard, Lady 77
Kennedy, Jacqueline _50_
Kennedy, John F. _50_
Kensington Palace 113
The King's Speech 11
Knight, Clara "Alla" 8

L
László, Philip de _6_
Laurence, Timothy 80
"Lillibet" 10
Logue, Lionel 11

M
McGuinness, Martin 124
Macmillan, Harold 46
Major, John 76
Malaysia 112
Malta 26, 28, 37
Mandela, Nelson 45
Marché Aux Fleurs Reine Elizabeth II _121_, 124
Margaret, Princess _16, 17, 18, 20_, 21, _81_
  birth 10
  childhood _3, 11_

death 89
divorce 61, 89
Marley, Rita 113
marriage 46, *83*
    children 26, 27, *28*
    engagement 21
    Golden Wedding 85
    honeymoon *24, 25*
    marriage certificate *24*
    procession *24*
    wedding 21, *23, 25, 25*
    wedding dress *22, 25, 25*
Mary, Queen 6, 9, *10*, 30
media coverage 52–3
Menzies, Robert 42
Middleton, Catherine *93*, 96, *96–7, 107, 108–09, 110*, 111, 112, *112–13*, 114, *114–15*
Millennium Dome *83*
Miller, Portia Simpson 112
Mitterrand, François *81*
modernization of the monarchy 85
Moore, Bobby 52, *52*
Mountbatten, Lord Louis 16, 26
    murder 59

N
New Zealand 8, 29, 36, 37, 38, 56, *56*, 91, 93, 113
Nkrumah, Kwame *41*, 44–5
Northern Ireland 57, 124
Nyerere, Julius 45

O
oath of allegiance *32*
Obama, Barack *98*
official birthday 52, 66
Order of the Garter 89, *94*
Order of the Thistle 89
Overseas Territories 36

P
Paki, Hori *56*
pantomime performances *8, 9*, 20–1
paparazzi 112
paperwork 86–7
Parker Bowles, Camilla 78, 87, 92, *108–09*, 117
Parliamentary reports 87
Party at the Palace 102, *124–5*
Philip, Prince 16, *20*, 21, *24, 25, 28*, 30, *33*, 42, 46, *46*, 50, *54–5*, 61, *83*, *104–05, 118–19, 122–23*
act of homage *32*
gaffes 73
Golden Wedding 85
health 100, 102
name 21
naval career 16, 26
title 25
World War II 16
Phillips, Autumn 106, *106*
Phillips, Isla 106
Phillips, Mark 57–8, *57, 60*, 78

Phillips, Mia 106
Phillips, Peter 57, *71*, 106, *106*, 120
Phillips, Savannah 106, *106*
Phillips, Zara *71, 73*, 106
    marriage *98*, 106
    sporting career 106
Pimlott, Ben 53
Pinsent, Matthew 102
portraits 6
postage stamps 50
press office 52, 56, 116
prime ministers 46–7, *47*, 59, 61, 70–1, *70*
    weekly audiences 87
Privy Council 47, *53*
Prom at the Palace 89, 91
public engagements 87

Q
Quayle, Dan 77

R
Ramphal, Shridath "Sonny" 45
Ramsey, Archbishop Michael 46
Reagen, Ronald *71*, 75
realms 36
Redgrave, Steven 102
regalia *30, 31, 33*
Regent's Park bandstand bomb 67
Remembrance Day 52
Republic of Ireland 59, 98–9, *100*, 124
republicanism 47, 50, 77, 109, 112, 124
Rhodesia crisis 45
Robinson, Peter *122–3*, 124
Roosevelt, Eleanor 16
Royal Ascot 52, *84–5*
Royal Family documentary 52–3, *53, 54–5*
royal finances 76
Royal Variety Performance *62–3*
Royal Windsor Horse Show 120

S
St Giles' Cathedral 89
St Paul's Cathedral
    Charles' wedding 67, *68–9*
    Diamond Jubilee service 102
    Golden Jubilee service 91
    Silver Jubilee service 57
Salmond, Alex *92*
Sandringham 15, 20, 26, 29, 71, 100, 114
Scotland *79*, 89
    independence movement 116
Scottish Parliament *92*
security breaches 66
Serjeant, Marcus 66
ship launchings 21, *21*
Silver Jubilee 57, *61, 62–5*
Simpson, Wallis 11, 15, 20, 58, *58*
    death 58
Singapore 112

Smith, Graham 109
Smith, Ian 45
Snowdon, Lord 61, 89
Solomon Islands 112
South Africa 20, 21, 36, *45*, 70
    withdrawal from Commonwealth *40*
Soviet Union 75, 76
Spencer, Lady Diana *see* Wales, Princess of
State Opening of Parliament *48*, 51–2
Scottish *92*
state visits 73, 86
    1947 South Africa *20*, 21, 36
    1951 Canada and Washington 28
    1952 Australia, New Zealand and Kenya 29, 36
    1953–4 Commonwealth Tour 36–42, *37, 38–9*
    1954 Australia 40, 42
    1961 Ghana 40, *41*, 44–5
    1961 India *43*, 44
    1970 Australia and New Zealand 56, *56*
    1972 France 58, *58*
    1983 India 73
    1983 United States 74
    1986 China 73, 75
    1991 United States 76
    1992 Australia 77
    1995 South Africa 45
    2000 Vatican 86, *87*
    2002 Golden Jubilee year 91–2
    2007 United States *95*
    2009 Canada 93
    2011 Australia 40, 99–100
    2011 Republic of Ireland 98–9, *100*
    2014 France 120, *121*, 124
    2015 Germany *118–19*, 122
Streisand, Barbara 59
Sturgeon, Nicola 116, *122–23*
succession rules changed 100, 114
Suez crisis 62
Swaziland 42

T
Teresa, Mother *73*
Thames river pageant 102, *102–3*
Thatcher, Margaret 45, 61, 70–1, *70*, 76
Thistle Service 89
three-day week 61
Tindall, Mike *98*, 106
Tonga *37*, 42
train, royal 87
Trooping the Colour 52
    shots fired during 66, *66*
Truman, Harry S. 28
Tuvalu 36, 112

U
Uganda 37

United Nations address 93, *93*
United States 17, 18, 76, 91
    Queen addresses Congress 76, *77*

V
Verwoed, Hendrik *40*
Victoria, Queen 58, 100, 102, 116
Viner, Vic 102

W
Wales, Prince of *see* Charles, Prince
Wales, Princess of 66–7, *68–9*, 70, *71, 73*, 75, 77
    death 80–1, *82–3*, 85
    walkabouts *45*, 56, 57
Westminster Abbey
    Anne's wedding 57
    coronation 30
    Elizabeth's wedding 21, *23*, 25
    funeral of the Queen Mother *88*
    William's wedding 96, *96*
William, Prince *71, 72, 73*, 92, 96, *96*, 102, 106, *107, 108–09, 111, 110*, 111, 112, *112, 114–15*
    charisma 92–3
    children 106–14, *107, 108–09, 110, 114–15*
    marriage *93*, 96, *96–7*
    military career 92
    Order of the Garter *94*
    state visits *93*, 112
    wedding 46
Wilson, Harold 46–7, *47*, 59, 61
Windsor, Duchess of *see* Simpson, Wallis
Windsor, Duke of *see* Edward VIII
Windsor Castle 20, 92
    fire 77, *78*, 80
Wonder, Stevie 102
World Cup, 1966 52, *52*
World War II 16–21, 25
    Auxiliary Territorial Service *19*, 21
    Children's Hour broadcast *16*, 17–18, *17*, 20
    victory celebrations 21

Y
yacht, royal 37, *72*
Yeomen of the Guard 51–2
York, Duchess of *see* Ferguson, Sarah
York, Duke of *see* Prince Andrew

Z
Zimbabwe 45

Picture Credits

The publishers would like to thank the following sources for their kind permission to reproduce the pictures in this book.

Corbis: /Bettmann: 37T; /Hulton-Deutsch Collection: 57; /Quadrillion: 128

The Dwight D. Eisenhower Library and Museum: 42

The Entertainment Artistes' Benevolent Fund: 62L, 62R, 63L, 63R, 64TL, 64BR

Getty Images: 46, 47, 67, 71T, 85BR, 87T, 88, 93, 95R; /AFP: 24BL, 44B, 91, 92, 98BL; /Carl Court /AFP: 102–103; /Gamma-Keystone: 25, 28L, 45TL; /Tim Graham: 40BL, 75, 77, 78, 79; /Hulton Archive: 8R, 9L, 22, 24T, 24BR, 48, 51BR; 54–55, 56, 59, 61B, 65, 70BR; /Samir Hussein /WireImage: 104–105; /Chris Jackson: 108–109, 111, 112–113, 114–115, 121; /Andrew Milligan: 122–123; /Max Mumby/Indigo: 107, 110; /Popperfoto: 3, 10, 14, 15T, 15BR, 20B, 33TR, 40–41, 43; /Stefano Rellandini/AFP: 120; /Murray Sanders: 117; /Julian Stratenschulte/AFP: 118–119; /Time & Life Pictures: 86; /WireImage: 89

Hardy Amies Archive: 61TR, 74

Imperial War Museum: 19

Mary Evans Picture Library: 7BL; /Illustrated London News Ltd: 8L, 28–29, 33TL, 34TL, 34TR, 34B, 35TL, 35B, 36TR, 36BR, 50, 52; /Imagno: 9R; /The Womens Library: 49

Mirrorpix: 12, 13

The National Archives, UK: 23, 29R

Press Association Images: /AP: 11, 20T, 21, 37B, 58TL, 66; /Fiona Hanson/PA Archive: 44TL, 83BR; /Anwar Hussein/Empics Entertainment: 72TL, 100TL; /Susannah Ireland/PA Archive: 5; /Chris Ison/PA Wire: 96–97; /Martin Keene/PA Archive: 45TR; /Doug Mills/AP: 76; /Yui Mok/ PA Wire: 99; /Neil Munns/PA Archive: 84–85; /PA Archive: 6, 16, 18, 27, 30TR, 30R, 33B, 38L, 40L, 51T, 53BR, 60, 68–69, 72B, 80–81, 82–83, 87BR; /Laurent Rebours/AP: 81TR; /John Stillwell/ AP: 100–101; /Topham Picturepoint: 7R; /Lewis Whyld/PA Wire: 98T

Private Collection: 70TL

REX Shutterstock: 53T, 71BR, 73, 94–95; /Nils Jorgensen: 124–125; /Ian MacDonald: 106; /Nicholas Read: 80L

St Paul's Cathedral: 90TL, 90TR, 90BL, 90BR

Topfoto: /Heritage-Images/The National Archives: 17; /Keystone Archives/HIP: 58B; /Public Record Office/HIP: 32

The UK Hydrographic Office: 38–39

Victoria and Albert Museum: /Cecil Beaton/V&A Images: 31

Every effort has been made to acknowledge correctly and contact the source and/or copyright holder of each picture and Carlton Books Limited apologises for any unintentional errors or omissions which will be corrected in future editions of this book.

Memorabilia Credits

Dwight D. Eisenhower Library and Museum, reproduced by permission of HM The Queen: 42
Entertainment Artistes' Benevolent Fund: 62–4
Getty Images: 95R; /Hulton Archive: 8r, 9l, 22, 24t
Hardy Amies Archive: 74
Mary Evans Picture Library: /Illustrated London News Ltd: 8l, 34–5; /Imagno: 9r
Mirrorpix.com: 12–3
National Archives, UK: 23, 29r
Private Collection: 70t
St Paul's Cathedral, the Dean and Chapter of: 90
TopFoto.co.uk/The National Archives/Heritage-Images: 17; /Public Record Office/HIP: 32
UK Hydrographic Office: 38–9

RIGHT The Queen takes a salute at Trooping the Colour in 1982.